INDEX
ON CENSORSHIP

INDEX ON CENSORSHIP 4 1995

Volume 24 No 4 July/August 1995   Issue 165

Editor & Chief Executive
Ursula Owen
Director of Administration
Philip Spender
Deputy Editor
Judith Vidal-Hall
Production Editor
Rose Bell
Fundraising Manager
Elizabeth Twining
News Editor
Adam Newey
Editorial Assistants
Anna Feldman
Philippa Nugent
Africa
Adewale Maja-Pearce
Eastern Europe
Irena Maryniak
Circulation & Marketing Director
Louise Tyson
Subscriptions Manager
Robin Jones

Directors
Louis Blom-Cooper, Ajay Chowdhury, Caroline Moorehead, Ursula Owen, Peter Palumbo, Jim Rose, Anthony Smith, Philip Spender, Sue Woodford (Chair)

Council
Ronald Dworkin, Amanda Foreman, Thomas Hammarberg, Clive Hollick, Geoffrey Hosking, Michael Ignatieff, Mark Littman, Pavel Litvinov, Robert McCrum, Uta Ruge, William Shawcross, Suriya Wickremasinghe

Patrons
Chinua Achebe, David Astor, Robert L Bernstein, Harold Evans, Richard Hamilton, Stuart Hampshire, Yehudi Menuhin, Iris Murdoch, Philip Roth, Stephen Spender, Tom Stoppard, Michael Tippett, Morris West

Australian committee
Philip Adams, Blanche d'Alpuget, Bruce Dawe, Adele Horin, Angelo Loukakis, Ken Methold, Laurie Muller, Robert Pullan and David Williamson c/o Ken Methold, PO Box 6073, Toowoomba West, Queensland 4350

Danish committee
Paul Grosen, Niels Barfoed, Claus Sønderkøge, Herbert Pundik, Nils Thostrup, Toni Liversage and Björn Elmquist, c/o Claus Sønderkøge, Utkaervej 7, Ejerslev, DK-7900 Nykobing Mors

Accountant
Suzanne Doyle
Volunteer Assistants
Michaela Becker
Daniel Brett
Laura Bruni
Nathalie de Broglio
Jason Garner
Kirsty Gordon
Joe Hipgrave
Colin Isham
Claudia Jessop
Jenny Liebscher
Anne Logie
Nevine Mabro
Nicholas McAulay
Jamie McLeish
Atanu Roy
Sarah Smith
Katheryn Thal
Henry Vivian-Neal

Dutch committee
Maarten Asscher, Gerlien van Dalen, Christel Jansen, Bert Janssens, Chris Keulemans, Frank Ligtvoet, Hans Rutten, Mineke Schipper, Steffie Stokvis, Martine Stroo and Steven de Winter, c/o Gerlien van Dalen and Chris Keulemans, De Balie, Kleine-Gartmanplantsoen 10, 1017 RR Amsterdam

Norwegian committee
Trond Andreassen, Jahn Otto Johansen, Alf Skjeseth and Sigmund Strømme, c/o NFF, Skippergt. 23, 0154 Oslo

Swedish committee
Ana L Valdés and Gunilla Abrandt, c/o *Dagens Nyheter*, Kulturredaktionen, S-105 15 Stockholm, Sweden

USA committee
Susan Kenny, Peter Jennings, Jeri Laber, Anne Nelson, Harvey J Kaye, Wendy Wolf, Rea Hederman, Jane Kramer, Gara LaMarche, Faith Sale, Michael Scammell

Cover design by Andrea Purdie

Index on Censorship (ISSN 0306-4220) is published bimonthly by a non-profit-making company: Writers & Scholars International Ltd, Lancaster House, 33 Islington High Street, London N1 9LH Tel: 0171-278 2313 Fax: 0171-278 1878 E-mail: indexoncenso@gn.apc.org http://www.oneworld.org/index oc/ Internet Gopher site: gopher.iia.org:70

Index on Censorship is associated with Writers & Scholars Educational Trust, registered charity number 325003

Second class postage (US subscribers only) paid at Irvington, New Jersey. Postmaster: send US address changes to *Index on Censorship* c/o Virgin Mailing & Distribution, 10 Camptown Road, Irvington, NJ 07111

Subscriptions 1995 (6 issues p.a.): £32 (overseas £38 or US$48). Students £24/US$36

© This selection Writers & Scholars International Ltd, London 1995
© Contributors to this issue, except where otherwise indicated

Printed by Martins, Berwick upon Tweed, UK

Cover pictures: John Bryson/Camera Press (front); Terry Smith/Camera Press (back and title page)

Former Editors: Michael Scammell (1972-81); Hugh Lunghi (1981-83); George Theiner (1983-88); Sally Laird (1988-89); Andrew Graham-Yooll (1989-93)

STEPHEN SPENDER

28 February 1909 — 16 July 1995

Word

The word bites like a fish.
Shall I throw it back free
Arrowing to that sea
Where thoughts lash tail and fin?
Or shall I pull it in
To rhyme upon a dish?

Stephen Spender

Just as we were sending the disk to the printer, news came of Stephen Spender's death at home in London on Sunday 16 July. He was the key founder of *Index on Censorship*, and stayed with it. He wrote for *Index*, fundraised for it, sat on its committees and introduced others into its work, gave poetry readings and travelled for it. In 1972 he welcomed Joseph Brodsky, then just out of the Soviet Union, into his home. After the Tiananmen Square massacre he helped the Chinese poet Liu Hong Bin. In 1992, looking at 20 years of *Index*, he wrote, 'The lesson of the twentieth century seems to be that "life is criticism of life", and that where criticism is suppressed by absolute government there is only death.' Even without his watchful and supportive presence, we shall keep his spirit alive in *Index*. Tributes will be published in the next issue. ❑
Poem published by kind permission of Faber and Faber

CONTENTS

EDITORIAL	6	**URSULA OWEN** Missing agenda
LETTER	8	**BOSNIA-HERCEGOVINA** Recipe for the UN
IN THE NEWS	9	**LAURA BRUNI** Romania: Living on the edge
	12	**CHARLES ARTHUR** Haiti: Fractured state
	15	**JUDITH VIDAL-HALL** Turkey: Enter the army
	17	**LINDSEY COLLEN** Mauritius: Mauritian mêlée
	19	**DULUE MBACHU** Nigeria: A dastardly business
	21	**LAURA BRUNI** Britain: The film they tried to kill
	23	**A SPECIAL CORRESPONDENT** Pakistan: Karachi action
INTERVIEW	25	**VLADIMIR GUSINSKY** The man with the Most money
COVER STORY	31	**THE BODY POLITIC**
	32	**NAILA KABEER** Selective rights, collective wrongs
	42	**SECRET ASIA** The baby gulag
	46	**ERICA JONG** Deliberately lewd
	50	**GUSTAVE COURBET** Unveiling the origin of the world
	51	**LUDMILA PETRUSHEVSKAYA** Panya's poor heart
	57	**IRENA MARYNIAK** Beauty goes East
	62	**HUMAN RIGHTS WATCH** No change
	64	**CAROLINE MOOREHEAD** Hostage to a male agenda
	72	**LEPA MLADJENOVIĆ** Where do I come from?
	76	**ON THE LINE**
	78	**EMMANUEL WOTANY** Thou shalt not suffer a witch
	81	**URVASHI BUTALIA** Hidden histories
	90	**RED DE MUJERES CONTRA LA VIOLENCIA** The wheel of power and control
	92	**TIBET WOMEN'S ASSOCIATION** A state-owned womb
	94	**UNESCO** Why women?
	95	**ANNA J ALLOT** 'If you can wait'
PHOTO FEATURE	96	**WEDDING IN KHOMEIN**
BABEL	102	**FELIX CORLEY** A small war you may have missed
MINORITIES	108	**VIRGINIA LULING** People of the clay
	113	**SURVIVAL** Third time lucky?

CONTENTS

COUNTRY FILE

- 115 **CUBA REDUX**
- 117 **ADAM NEWEY** No more heroes
- 123 **MARTHA GELLHORN** Forty years on
- 126 **MARTA BEATRIZ ROQUE CABELLO** Let's talk about the Cuban economy
- 129 **NÉSTOR BAGUER** Health for hard currency
- 132 **RICARDO REY DE LEÓN** Thou shalt respect thy President — and all his works
- 133 **NÉSTOR BAGUER** In search of an ethic
- 136 **YNDAMIRO RESTANO DÍAZ** Poem
- 137 **GUSTAVO ARCOS BERGNES** Whose army?
- 142 **ALBERTO ABREU ARCIA** Memory of a punishment
- 145 **ARIEL HIDALGO** Miami vices
- 151 **JOSÉ CONRADO RODRÍGUEZ** Out of the lie

DIARY

- 154 **MÁRTON MESTERHÁZI** Journey to Bled

LETTER FROM AFRICA

- 159 **ADEWALE MAJA-PEARCE** Zambia: Cautionary tales

LEGAL

- 163 **CHRISTOPHER HIRD** Rebuffed in Britain

INDEX INDEX

- 167 **FLASHPOINTS** China/Bahrain

The Trustees and Directors would like to thank
all those whose donations support *Index on Censorship* and
Writers and Scholars Educational Trust, including

The Noel Buxton Trust
Carlton Communications plc
Institusjonen Fritt Ord
The Goldberg Family Charitable Trust
The Lyndhurst Settlement
The Onaway Trust
The Royal Ministry of Foreign Affairs, Norway
SIDA (Swedish International Development Authority)

Index **and WSET depend on donations
to guarantee their independence and to fund research**

*From now on we shall be giving more regular prominence to our donors, whose support is so
essential to our work. A different list will be published in each issue*

EDITORIAL

Missing agenda

The UN's decision to hold the Fourth World Conference on Women in Beijing in September reflects rather more hypocrisies than usual. With its known aversion to free speech and debate — at least 2,000, some say tens of thousands, in its gaols — and the infamous treatment of its unwanted girl babies, China is hardly the obvious place for a conference on women.

Already the 36,000 women representing non-governmental organisations have been banished to a site 50 kilometres from the main conference in Beijing. Six Taiwanese women's groups have been banned from attending unless they register as part of the Chinese delegation. Eight women's organisations from Tibet and several from Hong Kong have also been barred; any discussion of coercive family-planning practices in Tibet have been removed from the agenda. After endless negotiating, some bargains have been struck. It will be crucial now to monitor the agreements with the Chinese authorities.

As to the conference itself — the official one, that is — some delegates are already saying that they fear the end result, far from setting the agenda for women's rights for the next millennium, will be a status quo document. The programme considers women very much from the perspective of their participation in development, perpetuating the tendency to see women solely as disembodied economic agents, particularly since the draft Platform for Action (from which NGOs were excluded until the final few days) is said to be weak on health and human rights.

Index sets out the agenda which will be missing from official Beijing — the violation of women's bodies and rights by cultural and family traditions, something which greatly affects prospects for development but which what Naila Kabeer calls 'development-speak' has done little to address.

After Srebrenica there is no escaping the scale of the West's failure. The catastrophe caused by endorsing the founding of nations within boundaries roughly drawn around history's unresolved tangle of religious and political roots was never going to be resolved by proposing weakly-policed limits to the drives of fratricidal war: they merely protracted the agony and discredited the would-be international lawgivers.

So deep in the mire, paths to sanity and decency are harder still to find, but on page 6 we print as worth our readers' attention the proposals of the Helsinki Citizens' Assembly's Balkan Project. ❑

Lady Chatterley's Lover came from Florence...

to the
Index Auction of Banned Books

6 November 1995
in aid of our associated charity Writers and Scholars Educational Trust

We need more donations to make this event a success
If you have books, manuscripts, letters, cartoons or other material relating to censorship or dissent and would like to help promote free speech please consider making a donation.

Donations already received include:

- A signed copy of the first privately printed edition of *Lady Chatterley's Lover*, signed by the author
- The manuscript of W H Auden's *Shield of Achilles*
- A rare 1938 edition of Radclyffe Hall's *The Well of Loneliness*
- A pirated Polish edition of *Animal Farm*
- A first edition (Olympia Press) of Maxwell Kenton's *Candy*
- A first edition of Henry Miller's *The Cosmological Eye*
- Signed copies of their own work donated by such writers as Ken Follett, Erica Jong, Allen Ginsberg and Michael Holroyd
- A selection of underground publications from Russia and Eastern Europe.

If you'd like to donate or buy anything, or if you would like any further information, please contact us.

33 Islington High Street
London N1 9LH

Telephone 0171 278 2313 Fax 0171 278 1878

LETTER

Recipe for the UN

**From Mary Kaldor, Chair, hCa, Klelija Balta, Director, hCa-Tuzla, Mient Jan Faber, Co-ordinator, hCa Balkan Project
PO Box 85893, 2508 CN,
The Hague, The Netherlands**

The dramatic events in Srebrenica and other UN-designated Safe Areas in Bosnia and Hercegovina expose the moral vacuum among today's political leaders. The UN has been utterly humiliated. The loss of the eastern enclaves means that it will be very difficult to reintegrate Bosnia-Hercegovina. The theory that the UN can regroup and defend the rump of Bosnia-Hercegovina fails to take into account both the increased vulnerability of Sarajevo, now that Bosnian Serb firepower can be concentrated there and the threat to the fragile federation between Croats and Muslims posed by the continuing war.

Helsinki Citizens' Assembly (hCa) International, together with hCa-Tuzla, once more urge the international community to stop its policy of appeasement and retreat and embark on a firm and robust line of action in order to protect the population.
1. The rapid reaction forces should be stationed, without delay, in all the Safe Areas and create an effective shield against any act of aggression; 2. Access to the Safe Areas (by air and road) should be enforced and kept open; 3. The refugees from Srebrenica (and other Safe Areas) should be protected by UNPROFOR on their flight as well as in the centres and areas where they will be accommodated. The city of Tuzla — an enormous refugee centre — should receive additional aid in large quantities; 4. The return of refugees to their homes should be facilitated. The French offer to retake Srebrenica should be considered very seriously so that UN forces could be reinstalled there; 5. The international community's military operations in BH should be conducted under the command of France and/or Britain, with a mandate of the UN Security Council. The mandate should comprise: protection of Safe Areas; territorial integrity of BH; full access for humanitarian aid and 'other' UN operations; return of refugees.

hCa-Tuzla has appealed to the people living in the Serbian-controlled areas of BH to protest against the outrageous attacks of the Bosnian-Serb army and to join the civic peace forces in the whole of Bosnia-Hercegovina.

In the end there can be no solution to the conflict without the political collapse of the Bosnian Serb regime and other extreme nationalists. hCa-Tuzla are inviting all like-minded people in Bosnia Hercegovina and in Europe to come to Tuzla in October on the 50th anniversary of the UN for the hCa assembly under the slogan 'Unite the citizens, unite the nations.' ❏

The editor welcomes letters and comments from all **Index** *readers*

IN THE NEWS

LAURA BRUNI

Living on the edge

Romani are the fastest growing ethnic group in eastern Europe, but their present status is severely threatened by government complicity in public prejudice

On 13 May, the day that Czech President Václav Havel paid tribute to Romani victims of Nazi genocide during the *Porajmos* (gypsy Holocaust), a Czech Roma man was brutally murdered in a racist attack on his home. That same weekend Ion Cioaba, the Romanian 'King of Romanies Everywhere', declared: 'The Romani lived far better under Ceaucescu. They had jobs and were able to raise children. Now they can hardly make ends meet.'

These events encapsulate the post-Communist situation for the Romani in eastern Europe: their past and present suffering is not often acknowledged; they face hostility from their fellow citizens and they are at the bottom of the social, economic and political heap. Nowhere is this situation worse than in Romania.

On 23 May in Bucharest, Romanian President Ion Iliescu opened the International Seminar of Tolerance with the words: 'The traditions of tolerance, of respect for fellow men, the acceptance of diversity, are specific features of the Romanian people.' In February and May respectively, the United Nations Committee on Economic, Social and Cultural Rights (CESCR) and Amnesty International published reports presenting a very different picture. According to the CESCR, there has been no real improvement in the treatment of Romani since 1989, and they suffer many forms of unofficial discrimination, particularly in schools and workplaces. Amnesty highlighted 'a nationwide pattern of police failure' to protect Romani from racist attacks. It also charged the police with complicity in attacks, assaulting Romani in detention, detaining them solely because of their ethnic origin, failing to properly investigate racist violence and harassing those who complain.

In Romania expressing contempt for *tigani* is common; indeed the word *tigani*, regarded by Romani as little more than a term of abuse, was recently voted by Parliament as their official designation. Most Romanians don't want Romani in Romania, and accuse them of blackening the country's image abroad, blaming them for rising crime and the black market. Such prejudice is fostered through the media by a powerful ultra-nationalist bloc. Local officials making decisions affecting Romani tend to be particularly prejudiced against them, a situation noted by both Amnesty and the CESCR.

There are around one and a half million Romani in Romania. Many are completely assimilated and prefer not to identify with the hated *tigani*. However, prejudice is not the only obstacle to improving their status. There is a very real tension between their desire to join mainstream society and their desire to maintain a separate identity. Many unassimilated Romani fear that any integration will inevitably destroy their traditions. Roma identity is based on a sense of 'otherness'; historical experience has taught them to be wary of the *gadze* (non-Romani) world which has treated them so cruelly. Up to the mid-nineteenth century, in the core Romanian principalities of Moldavia and Wallachia, Romani were slaves. In the twentieth century the *Porajmos* killed 36,000 Romanian Romani, and an intensive 'Romanianisation' programme emphasised to Roma and non-Roma alike the 'incompatibility' of traditional Roma culture and 'progressive' Romanian culture. Kristina Kruck of the Soros Roma Foundation argues that having been victims for many generations, Romani find it difficult to imagine themselves in any other role. When it comes to asserting their legal rights, many Romani fear that complaint will only worsen their situation.

So far this large but divided and impoverished minority has been unable to exercise any political clout. The root of the problem lies in the traditional organisation of Roma society which is based on caste identity. Romania's 17 Romani political parties, organised on caste lines, see each other as rivals, not allies. They are ineffective and most Romani don't vote for them, so the government can either ignore them or operate a divide-and-rule policy.

Unlike Romania's politically well-organised Hungarian minority which has the Hungarian government as an advocate, Romani have no ready-made champion for their cause. Consequently Romani tend to rely on international bodies such as the European Union and the Council for Security and Co-operation in Europe to exert pressure for change on the Romanian government. These bodies have started taking the Romani seriously partly because they fear their potentially large-scale emigration westwards in search of a better life. Western policy now promotes Romani integration into Romanian society, pushing the government to boost their educational and employment opportunities so that they will no longer want to leave.

Few east European countries yet recognise that racist discrimination and violence against Romani are ➤

> **The traditions of tolerance, of respect for fellow men, are specific features of the Romanian people.**
>
> **Ion Iliescu, May 1995**

IN THE NEWS: ROMANIA

major social problems. Only in the Czech Republic has the growing incidence of racist violence prompted the government to pursue a tougher line. Even the Czechs are hardly 'Roma-friendly'; a proposed new law drafted in 1993 would effectively deprive most Romani of the possibility of proving Czech citizenship (*Index* 4&5/1994). During a 1994 seminar on Roma in Warsaw, Max Van der Stoel, CSCE High Commissioner on National Minorities, warned that if authorities tolerate racism they erode public confidence in the law and make minorities feel even less part of mainstream society.

Amnesty's report seriously embarrassed the Romanian government which hoped to use the seminar to showcase its progress since the December 1989 revolution. Romania joined the Council of Europe in 1993 (and has now formally applied for EU membership) on the strength of promises that it would deal effectively with its minority problems and govern according to the rule of law. So far it has failed to do either. But the West needs to do more than issue critical reports. Unless international bodies take the implications of their research seriously, Romani will remain on the margins of the new Romania. ❑

Romania: Broken Commitments to Human Rights (Amnesty International, May 1995, 44pp)
The Situation of Human Rights in Romania (United Nations Committee on Economic, Social and Cultural Rights, February 1995)

CHARLES ARTHUR

Fractured state

In the face of widespread criticism, President Aristide and the US embassy are making common cause in defence of the June election

Haiti's parliamentary and local council elections, which began on 25 June, were supposed to be a celebration of a democracy restored by the United Nations. But with international observers reporting cases of ballot burning, ballot stuffing, threats against electoral officials and a rise in political violence, both the United States and the Aristide government are struggling to establish the credibility of the electoral process.

The Clinton administration, through its embassy in Port-au-Prince acknowledged considerable irregularities in the poll but drew attention to the relatively low level of violence compared with past elections. President Aristide praised the maturity and calmness of the electorate in the face of logistical problems. His Lavalas party is expected to win a majority of the 2,000 seats up for election, after the second round of voting, now postponed until August, in areas where irregularities prevented electors from voting. The small right-wing parties that supported the military coup against Aristide in 1991 are predictably claiming the election is rigged, but more damaging are similar accusations by former allies, including the centre-left National Front for Change and Democracy (FNCD).

The FNCD, which supported Aristide in 1990, this time fielded candidates to stand against the Lavalas party. The split is interpreted as a result of friction between Aristide and FNCD leader, Evans Paul, who many believe is being groomed by the US as Aristide's successor as president. The FNCD showed scant regard for fair play, sowing confusion among a largely illiterate electorate by appropriating the slogans and symbols associated with Aristide's 1990 triumph.

In Port-au-Prince it was hard to find anyone with a good word for what appeared to be an election mainly for the benefit of a foreign audience. One man I spoke to said: 'What's the point in spending millions on elections when what we need is food and work?' and few people even knew the names of the candidates or the location of polling stations.

The low-key campaign and the evident lack of interest amongst voters was reflected in a turnout probably somewhat lower than the 50 per cent estimated by observers from the Organisation of American States. Whether the elections are finally deemed free and fair or not, the whole question of democracy in Haiti is overshadowed by the three years of military rule and the UN/US intervention which brought it to an end last October.

When Father Aristide entered the 1990 presidential election race at the head of a left and centre coalition, millions of Haitians who had previously played no part in electoral politics registered to vote for the first time. Vowing to break the power of the Duvalierists, and to resist interference by the United States, Aristide was the overwhelming choice of Haiti's poor. His victorious campaign was a joyful affair marked by massive rallies and demonstrations, and an unparalleled dialogue between politicians and electorate. The Haitian military, with money from the local elite and a nod and a wink from the US Embassy, intervened to nip this nascent participatory democracy in the bud. The peasant organisations, neighbourhood associations, and progressive Catholic groups, the backbone of Aristide's support, suffered intense and violent persecution.

That the Haitian people paid a heavy price for daring to vote for radical change is clear and goes some way towards explaining current disbelief in the value of elections. What has happened since the UN/US invasion has led some of Aristide's supporters to suggest that, although General Cédras and his army are gone, the attempt to eradicate Haiti's special brand of people's democracy continues.

In the more remote towns and villages, US Special Forces (who make up nearly half of the 6,000-strong UN force in Haiti) have been involved in a string of incidents that have violated the rights of Haitian civilians. Partisan actions by US troops, together with their failure to disarm the paramilitaries, are persuading many activists not to resume their political work because they fear for their safety.

Less obvious, but perhaps more damaging in the long run, is the influence of numerous US agencies, now well established throughout the country. Foremost among them is the Agency for International Development (AID). Critics say it is distributing millions of dollars to fund seemingly beneficial development projects with the aim of dividing and disrupting established local self-help organisations.

Also conspicuous during the lead-up to the elections were the International Republican Institute and the Centre for Free Enterprise and Democracy. In the name of 'democracy enhancement', these groups and others are trying to create anti-Lavalas party structures that can exploit the increasingly fractured state of Aristide's 1990 coalition.

With the streets of Port-au-Prince jammed with the vehicles of the UN military and countless other international organisations there is a real sense of Haiti being a country under occupation. The feeling that decisions are being made not by the elected government but by planners in New York and Washington is nowhere more apparent than in the difference between the Aristide who was elected in 1990 and the Aristide who returned to the National Palace last October.

Although he has done away with the reviled Haitian military, which will be replaced by a US-trained police force, the rest of Aristide's 1990 programme seems to have vanished without trace. There has yet to be one prosecution for the thousands of human rights violations committed during the coup years; and Aristide continues to preach reconciliation between bitter enemies. His government, far from being open and receptive to the demands of popular grassroots organisations, is distant and aloof, seemingly in the thrall of foreign advisers.

The view of the left-wing National Popular Assembly (APN), reflected in the influential weekly *Haïti Progrès*, is that once Aristide asked the US military to intervene on his behalf it was inevitable that any real progressive change would be vetoed.

Yet even if many on the Haitian left believe that Aristide has 'gone over to the other side', among the slum dwellers and peasants his popularity endures. The authority that Aristide still wields over the Haitian masses may well encourage the US to do what seemed unthinkable last year, and pressure him to stay on as president for three more years. Without him, all their plans for a stable and investment-friendly Haiti might unravel. ❑

Charles Arthur *edits* Haiti Briefing, *the newsletter of the London-based Haiti Support Group*

JUDITH VIDAL-HALL

Enter the army

Despite opposition from the army, Prime Minister Tansu Çiller has vowed to move ahead with plans to expand democracy in Turkey

On 30 June, in the course of a rare press briefing, the deputy Chief of the Turkish General Staff, General Ahmet Çörekçi, propounded the army's opposition to proposals on constitutional amendments now being debated in Parliament. In particular, he stressed, it could not contemplate the removal of Article Eight — the infamous anti-terrorism law, frequently used to silence critics of the government's treatment of its 12 million Kurds. (*Index* 1/1995). Humanitarian concerns, he continued, were an obstacle to the army's declared intention of ridding the country of the separatist Kurdish Workers Party (PKK), adding that the army was equally opposed to any political solution to the Kurdish problem. Concessions to the cultural claims of the Kurdish minority were, he said, like slicing a salami — 'The more you cut, the more they want.'

Press reaction to General Çörekçi's briefing were swift. 'Democracy and human rights are the norm, as is the subordination of military to civilian authority,' claimed one editorial; *Hürriyet* and *Milliyet*, both representative of the nationalist right, stressed the need to develop a democratic, civil society. It did not escape comment that such interventions had, in the past, been the precursor to the army's direct intervention in the political process. In other words, a military coup, the fourth since 1960, was not unthinkable.

Political reactions were, on the whole, predictable. Cem Boyer, leader of the opposition New Democracy Movement (YDH), claimed that had his party been in power, he would have sent the general packing. The leader of the social democrat Republican People's Party (CHP), in coalition with the government on condition that Article Eight is repealed, was more cautious, observing only that any decision on the matter was properly 'the business of Parliament'.

Which 'business', already stalled by party political rivalries, will not be any easier given the army's view. Changes in the 1982 constitution bequeathed by the army, need a two-thirds majority. The failure to achieve this cannot simply be laid at the door of the main opposition parties, particularly the Motherland Party (ANAP) whom the prime minister has accused of sabotaging her plans for reform. Though in principle most parties favour the amendments, even in the prime minister's own True Path Party (DYP) there is a core of die-hard conservatives, led by President Suleyman Demirel, opposed to any change. Furthermore, as Nicole Pope wrote in *Index* in January this year, 'most of the main parties were paralysed by infighting, rivalry between leaders prevented a union of like-minded parties on the right and the left, and few laws made it through a Parliament clearly more preoccupied with perks than with matters of state.'

Only seven of the 24 proposed changes got anywhere near the 300 votes required in the first round of voting on constitutional reforms; the second round of voting was due to begin in mid-July. One of the seven that did get through was that proposing the removal of a section in the preamble to the constitution praising the 1980 military coup.

The options left to Tansu Çiller in the face of the army's statement have narrowed. She can take a chance and go to the country, trusting in the Turkish voting public, many of whom, especially the younger generation, welcome change, and a 1994 opinion poll showing 86 per cent of the population in favour of a political solution to the Kurdish problem. In her address to her own party on 7 July, she said, 'No-one should be in any doubt that Turkey will become a more liberal, civil society...with greater respect for the individual and fully integrated with the rest of the modern world.' The economy remains fragile but an election/referendum on a European, democratising platform could win Çiller a majority. But while ANAP, formerly the main opposition party has had its political wings clipped, both the Islamist Welfare Party (RP), fortified by its huge success in the 1994 municipal elections and now reckoned the leading party nationally, and the army remain forces to be reckoned with.

Meanwhile, on 5 July, the army resumed its offensive against Kurdish guerrillas within the UN safe haven in northern Iraq. Since its initial incursion into northern Iraq in pursuit of PKK fighters on 19 March, the Turkish army has occupied a swathe of territory along the Turkish-Iraqi border. Despite Turkish claims to have withdrawn the bulk of its 35,000-strong invasion force, Kurdish sources claim a substantial number remain inside Iraq. Up to 3,000 Iraqi Kurds are reported to be fleeing from the Turkish advance.

The Turkish army are confident that by forestalling what they claim is a significant build-up of PKK forces within Iraq, they can bring their ferocious campaign in Turkish Kurdistan to a successful military conclusion. It puts the death toll this year at 19,000; other sources claim the figure is higher with wholesale evictions and destruction of villages still continuing.

While Turkey is a partner in the allied Operation Provide Comfort designed to protect Iraqi Kurds against Saddam Hussein, it would prefer to see the area returned to Iraqi jurisdiction and has been a leading lobbyist for the removal of UN sanctions against Baghdad. ❑

LINDSEY COLLEN

Mauritian mêlée

Caught between rival Hindu and Muslim fundamentalism, free speech in Mauritius is in danger of falling victim to the struggle for economic and political power between contending factions

The attacks by Muslim fundamentalists against Namassiwayam Ramalingum and his paper, *L'Indépendant* (*Index* 3/1995), illustrate only one aspect of a more widespread malaise in Mauritian society.

Mauritius has seen vast changes over the past 15 years. Since 1979, it has been paraded as one of the IMF and World Bank's economic 'success stories'.

Socially it is a different story: the island, best known as an idyllic resort for international tourists, has become tense and ill-at-ease with itself.

A road accident in May on the main motorway just outside the capital, Port Louis, for example, led to six hours of rioting. It was directed against any form of authority in sight and even when they opened fire on the rioters, the police had difficulty controlling the mob. Within hours, the riot showed signs of developing into a communal affair. The Hindu-Muslim divide that forms the basis of communalism here as in India, is increasingly taking on a fundamentalist tone. This dual-fundamentalism is further complicated by the presence of a substantial Christian community.

Tensions between communities have been exacerbated in recent years by political and economic factors.

The June state visit of the leader of the Indian opposition, Atal Bihari Vajpayee, leader of the fundamentalist Bharatiya Janata Party (BJP), combined official tours of state institutions with visits to a number of Hindu religious organisations. The Mauritian government was involved in planning this unprecedented mix of official and personal meetings.

The growth of the Muslim fundamentalist party, the Hisbullah, has been accompanied by increased political activity. A series of demands on the political front culminated in its denunciation of *L'Indépendant* for alleged attacks on the Prophet and threats of violence against its editor. The paper's demands for the liberalisation of meat imports had more to do with economics than religion.

The hierarchy of the Catholic Church of Mauritius is conservative to a degree. It is one of the few institutions in the world never to have taken a stand against apartheid; the Bishop's Lent message took issue with the government tax on the sugar barons. It has recently refused to implement anti-discrimination regulations on staffing and students in the schools it controls but which depend on public funding.

But growing communal feeling and the various fundamentalisms conceal more crude conflicts. The switch to economic privatisation means great prizes are to be had. Those in the running are different sections of a ruthless bourgeoisie.

Not everyone can win and privatisation means conflict as goods and services recently owned and controlled by the state are handed over to the 'old' money represented by just a few families, usually the ones that owned and controlled them before independence, before universal suffrage.

Other would-be winners in the privatisation handout can succeed only to the extent that they can enlist the deadly 'isms' on their side. This is all-out war for the enrichment of a few.

Fed with propaganda about Mauritius' success — a model for Africa, the tiger of the Indian Ocean and so on — most Mauritians wonder what's going on. All they see of the Mauritian miracle is the growing spectre of increasingly insecure jobs, sweatshop conditions, compulsory overtime as low-paid factory workers (US$100 a month), prices no longer controlled, sugar mills closing down, a housing shortage, threats of privatised health, education, electricity and water.

So what do the attacks on *L'Indépendant,* supposedly unleashed by outraged Muslim sensibilities, have to do with all this? The paper, the precise ownership of which remains unclear, represents the interests of one group competing in the privatisation stakes who thought to advance its cause by taking over the Ministry of Finance, the department in charge of privatisation. In its bid for the political power that would give them the economic edge, it had no scruples about manipulating Hindu and Tamil communalism.

L'Indépendant combined scurrilous rumours with some genuine exposés of important financial scandals — both of which led to an increase in its circulation. It was equally up front in its defence of 'Hindu power'; many felt that the victims of its character assassinations were often chosen because they were Muslims. The newspaper also carried scurrilous attacks against me and my novel *The Rape of Sita* (Index 4&5/1994).

None of which warrants the violence unleashed against the paper by Muslim extremists: public burnings, public threats, fire-bombs at the printers. These were followed a week later by the equally disturbing spectacle of orators defending *L'Indépendant* burning three other newspapers — *L'Express*, *Le Mauricien* and *Le Mag* — for being 'anti-Hindu'. The mainstream press is still effectively owned and controlled by a Euro-centred Catholic elite. This burning of newspapers took place at the celebration of a religious festival at a new building called 'Hindu House' and in the presence of official advisers to the prime minister. One of the first organisations to be associated with this new Hindu centre was the Hindu Business Council.

> The Hindu-Muslim divide that forms the basis of communalism, is increasingly taking on a fundamentalist tone

While communalism and fundamentalism have been enlisted to serve the economic interests of the few, for the majority they represent the politics of despair. In March, however, the Movement Against Communalism (MAC) was founded to counteract this madness. It is potentially strong, including the whole of the trade union movement, consumers' groups, environmentalists, the women's movement, almost all musicians in the country, pre-school playgroup organisers, adult literacy groups, a health co-operative, an agricultural organisation, and an organisation of the blind — as well as many individuals. MAC rejects all forms of classification or categorisation of people along communal, ethnic or religious lines. It exposes institutionalised communalism — in laws, in organisational forms — and opposes all links between organised religions and politics. And it defends freedom of expression.

The vested interests that resort to communalism, racism and religious strife are, among so much else, the enemies of free expression. ❏

Lindsey Collen was born in South Africa and is now based in Mauritius. Her first novel, There is a Tide, *was published in 1990*

DULUE MBACHU

A dastardly business

Despite protests from western governments on the conduct of the proceedings, the trials of alleged coup plotters continues in secret in Nigeria

The continuing story of a supposed plot to overthrow Abacha has proved particularly intriguing in recent months. In late February, a number of independent publications reported that some military officers had been arrested on suspicion of subversion. The army information department denied the reports, saying that a few officers were merely being questioned for spreading 'rumours and disaffection'. Shortly afterwards, the military authorities were singing a different tune: a coup plot had indeed been uncovered and 29 officers and civilians were under investigation.

The investigations took an unusually long time by Nigerian standards and, at one point, the London *Observer* reported that scores of non-commissioned officers had been executed near the capital, Abuja, in connection with the alleged plot — to the vehement denials of the military authorities, whose spokesman decried the story as 'wicked'. Some newspapers even came to the conclusion that there had been no plot at all. Nonetheless, in March, Abacha himself publicly indicted the former head of state, General Olusegun Obasanjo, saying that he was 'personally embarrassed' when security reports indicated Obasanjo's complicity in such 'a dastardly act'.

The trials of the plotters eventually began in a military court on 5 June, when the press was allowed to photograph the handcuffed suspects as they listened to the charges against them but entered no pleas. The trials have since continued in secret and were due to conclude by the end of June. However, reports that Obasanjo has already been sentenced to a lengthy prison term, and other defendants sentenced to death, are being vigorously denied by the government.

Concurrent with the trial, mass arrests and detention without trial, the stock-in-trade of General Sani Abacha's regime, reached a new peak in the run-up to the second anniversary of the annulment of the presidential election of 12 June 1993. Alhaji Wada Nas, Abacha's minister for special duties, raised the spectre of a plot by pro-democracy activists to disturb the peace in commemoration of the election; a few days later, on 31 May, a bomb exploded at an official function killing five people and injuring more than 20 others.

No-one claimed responsibility for the blast, and if the blast was aimed at Mariam Abacha, absent from the function at which she was expected, it failed. But, as if on cue, security operatives swung into action, picking up all known critics of military rule. Among those arrested was Chief Michael Ajasin, the 87-year-old leader of the National Democratic Coalition (NADECO), along with about 70 of his members. The information minister, Dr Walter Ofonagoro, told the BBC that 'there is nothing democratic in an octogenarian planting bombs.' In the event, however, Ajasin was only accused of holding an illegal meeting and, after spending the night at a police station, was allowed to go home.

Many human rights activists were also hauled in for questioning; some were locked up, others released. On the eve of 12 June, one report claimed that over 200 pro-democracy activists had been arrested in the preceding fortnight.

Nor were journalists spared: Kunle Ajibade, editor of the *News*, Ben Charles Obi, editor of *Weekend Clasique*, George Mbah, an assistant editor with *Tell* magazine, and Chris Anyanwu, publisher of the *Sunday Magazine*, were all arrested around the same time and are being held at the Directorate of Military Intelligence (DMI). On 8 June, the attorney-general's office announced the extension for another six months of the proscription of two newspaper houses: the Concord group, owned by Moshood Abiola, the winner of the annulled 1993 elections, and the Punch group. It is generally believed that, when the current proscription of the Guardian newspaper group runs out in August, that will also be extended. ❑

Dulue Mbachu *is a journalist with the Lagos-based* African Guardian, *currently banned*

LAURA BRUNI

The film they tried to kill

The commercial release, in June, of a video containing live archive footage of executions, provoked a knee-jerk outburst in the British press and sent it to the top of the video hit parade

Reactions to *Executions*, a video documentary on capital punishment, which were in general ill-informed and, in many cases, from people who it turned out had either not seen the film or, on reflection, decided they had seen something else, were almost universally opposed to the film's production. They ranged from standard right-on outrage from the morally shocked and disgusted, to broadsheet editorials mainly concerned with the fact that someone might actually make money out of a video purporting to educate people on the evils of the death penalty.

In the event, the furore achieved precisely the opposite from its intentions: the video shot up the ratings list to number one, knocking *Schindler's List* off its long-held perch. *Index* staff watched it, decided it was a serious document, and wondered just what all the fuss was about. The only 'shocking' element was the subject itself: the continuing use — now spreading — of legal execution, often for no more than daring to speak out against tyranny.

We present below a brief chronology of events, starting with the difficulties encountered by the makers of *Executions* in getting access to publicly-held archive footage, and ask the more serious question: who controls the use of public documents?

November 1994 The production company Still Movements is commissioned by Eduvision Ltd to produce a documentary film *Executions*, a history of capital punishment in the twentieth century. Still Movements have full editorial control and insist that a percentage of any profits go to a human rights campaigning organisation.
December Still Movements and Eduvision ask Amnesty International for access to Amnesty's research facilities and help with locating footage. They also ask Amnesty for a letter outlining its stance on a video about executions.
8 January 1995 Letter to Eduvision from Amnesty: 'We share your objective of raising public awareness about the shocking phenomenon of executions that take place around the world... The historical analysis of the context of the technology of execution can make an important contribution to the debate on the death penalty...'
26 January Still Movements send an outline detailing the use to which film in the Imperial War Museum's extensive film archive of war crimes will be put and justifying the intended use of shocking images. 'There is no other way to show the reality of capital punishment than to show cap-

A SPECIAL CORRESPONDENT

ital punishment.' The IWM agrees to release VHS viewing copies of requested footage, but tells David Monaghan of Still Movements: 'We are concerned about your intended means of distribution and feel strongly that normal retail outlets will not reach your intended audience.'

31 January Letter from Amnesty to Eduvision: 'I understand from our meeting that you are prepared to allow us full editorial control... I must express concern with a number of aspects of the proposed marketing of this project... I am disturbed by the proposal to feed "shocking images" to the "tabloid newspapers" with the aim of making this the "most talked about subject at many after dinner parties"... I also question the proposed choice of W H Smith as distributor.'

17 February Letter from Amnesty to co-producer David Herman informing him that Amnesty has withdrawn from the project completely: 'It would be naive not to acknowledge that any support from Amnesty, be it tacit or implicit, will give this video a credibility it might otherwise lack. Indeed, as far as I can see, our support is required even to access much of the material, reflecting the concern of the Imperial War Museum and Reuters that it should not be used or distributed in an inappropriate context.'

20 February Fax from IWM to David Monaghan: 'In the light of Amnesty International's total withdrawal of support for your video project and the concern they have expressed over the possibility of the subject being sensationalised, we too now feel this is something we do not wish to be involved with. Therefore no further material will be supplied to you for your project.'

The disputed footage was eventually acquired from US archives and from private collections in the UK; and on 5 May, *Executions* was finally submitted to the British Board of Film Classification (BBFC).

15 June BBFC gives *Executions* an 18 certificate with only minor cuts to final sequence.

16 June Executions released through mainstream video outlets.

18 June News of the World publishes article headlined 'BAN IT! Sick execution video that W H Smith is happy to sell' and challenges the store to remove the video.

19 June One MP condemns the video as 'a 55-minute peep show of violent death'.

W H Smith issues a statement announcing that *Executions* will be withdrawn from sale.

BBFC director James Ferman issues a statement supporting the award of an 18 certificate: 'the video was felt to be within the range of discourse, polemical or otherwise, which adults in a free society should be entitled to view.'

21 June An *Independent* editorial questions the appropriateness of such a film being sold on the commercial market.

Gerald Kaufman MP attacks *Executions* in the *Daily Telegraph* questioning Ferman's decision to certify the video and questions why it is being sold in the UK which has abolished the death penalty.

25 June The *Independent on Sunday* publishes an article outlining Amnesty's original support for the project, alleging that discussions broke down when Amnesty asked for full editorial control.

Martin Baker, head of the School of Cultural Studies, University of the West of England, issues a four-page report on the construction of the video and the way in which it puts its arguments forward, concluding that it should be classed as a serious documentary with an intentional capacity to disturb. He concludes: 'It is sadly not uncommon to dismiss as "outrageous" and "shocking" and "dangerous" the powerful presentation of arguments with which people disagree.' ❑

A SPECIAL CORRESPONDENT

Karachi action

The Pakistan government draws close to repeating past errors

There is a civil war going on in Karachi with law enforcement agencies pitted against the supporters of the Mohajir Qaumi Movement (MQM). Given the overwhelming support for the party's leader, Altaf Hussein, this means virtually the whole of the 5-6 million Mohajir community in this city of 11 million.

The recent escalation of violence

A SPECIAL CORRESPONDENT

— more than 1,000 dead this year, over 400 in the last six weeks — is overwhelmingly the result of the government's latest offensive to crush the MQM as an organised political force (*Index* 3/1995).

Well-armed Mohajir dissidents, the Haqiqi, operate in collusion with the police and the paramilitary Rangers. Ten-twenty people, mostly innocent civilians, are killed every day. Districts of Karachi like Orangi, Landhi and Korangi are under siege, their inhabitants arrested, tortured and butchered at random.

The government's aim, it appears, is to convince the Mohajirs that if they continue to support Altaf Hussein they can expect no peace in the city. If it can prolong its operation in the city for long enough, it reasons, Hussein will find himself isolated, and a new leadership, willing to collaborate with the government, will emerge.

The government-MQM talks in Islamabad in mid-July, intended to convince the world that the government is serious about restoring peace in Karachi, look like a charade. Altaf Hussein is presented in the official media as a terrorist out to wreck the state; the prime minister continues to treat Karachi as an isolated 'law and order' problem that will be resolved if sufficient force is employed.

Daily, individuals claiming to be MQM terrorists, confess to a range of crimes they have committed under Hussein's instructions. One of them, an MQM senator, who had mysteriously disappeared from Peshawar Central Jail where he was being held on unproved charges, was produced two days later on television, in police custody, where he made a full and frank confession of multiple acts of terrorism, all at the direction of the MQM leader.

For many older Pakistanis, such methods are all too reminiscent of the time when victims of Awami League 'terrorism' were produced on Pakistan TV, and the Bengali leader, Sheik Mujibur Rahman, was removed from East Pakistan (now Bangladesh) and tried for sedition, in the hope a new leadership with whom the military government could deal would emerge.

In 1971, media propaganda succeeded in turning the overwhelming majority of West Pakistan's citizens against the Bengalis: they approved the military government's action in the Eastern province — and lost it to Mujib and the Awami League. Today, critics of Benazir Bhutto's action in Karachi are growing in number. ❑

Find Index at:

http://www.oneworld.org/index_oc/

VLADIMIR GUSINSKY

The man with the Most money

One of Russia's richest, but by no means most favoured, sons talks of storm-troops and future shock in an interview with *Index*'s Irena Maryniak

Vladimir Gusinsky, marked man, prototycoon, hustler and plutocrat *extraordinaire*, proved to be a mild-mannered, bespectacled figure, dapper in his grey suit, swift speaking and with a tendency to blush. The leather jacket and dark glasses, at one time his much trumpeted trademark, are gone — and there's not a bodyguard in sight. A chameleon perhaps? Four months of self-imposed exile, after a bout of rough treatment from Boris Yeltsin's personal security guards, and the camouflage is complete. His London office is discreetly placed down a long, pale corridor on the fourth floor of the City Tower, nightmarishly lined with unmarked doors.

This is the man reputed to be one of Russia's pushiest media barons, the founder and head of the Most Group (42 operating companies, including a bank and 10 property firms), the owner of Russia's first private television station (NTV) and liberal newspaper (*Segodnya*), and with a controlling interest in the popular radio station, *Ekho Moskvy*. He is currently negotiating with the Bank of England to set up an affiliate in London. His net personal fortune is estimated at US$50 million, but his operating assets run into many billions: among other things, he manages Moscow city's finances. A meteoric rise for a former trainee in theatrical production, but how did he do it?

'Actually it's very simple,' he confides disarmingly. 'When one political structure crumbles and another takes its place, huge lacunae appear. People who can sense their outline and organise themselves and others to slip into the space can achieve great things. Social tremors can generate considerable wealth. Our country offers high profits; but can lose everything in an instant.'

Gusinsky's background is impeccably heterogeneous for a banker straddling the economic divide between East and West. Parents on either side of the revolutionary divide: mother from a well-to-do bourgeois family with a labour camp record to its credit; father a Ukrainian-Jewish factory worker. Gusinsky's childhood was sprayed with routine bursts of anti-Semitism — a strengthening experience, he says. In a country with currently over 100 extreme-right and fascist publications, some running articles alleging a Jewish plot to conquer Russia, how does his background serve him now?

'I wouldn't peddle my nationality. Extreme fascist organisations do exist in Russia and their publications are not regulated in any way, even though in theory legal controls are in place. All the authorities do is make pious declarations or indulge in demonstrative gestures intended to show that fascism is here to terrorise us all. This is directed at the West to justify arbitrary actions that are not dictated by any political necessity.'

Gusinsky has been the victim of arbitrary initiatives himself. Last December, he was followed to his office by a group of masked thugs armed with sniper rifles who subsequently ransacked the Most Bank headquarters and forced Gusinsky's security men to lie in the snow for several hours. The attackers were presidential security men answerable to the head of the presidential security service, General Aleksandr Korzhakov, a tenebrous presence behind Boris Yeltsin who performs the dual role, it is said, of personal bodyguard and bosom friend. Gusinsky left the country. A criminal case was brought against the presidential security service employees involved and recently dropped. If found guilty, they could have faced up to 10 years' imprisonment.

Just why Gusinsky was targeted for attack is a moot and thorny question. He puts it down to his refusal to co-operate in a proposed financial deal — on which he refuses to elaborate further — and to promote government policy in his sector of the media. 'I didn't want to be court banker to the powers that be. There's money I want and there's money that stinks. I told them I wanted to go on making money my way. I want to feel that Russia is a country in which I may or may not be liked by the president's bodyguard, but I shouldn't be afraid of opening the post or of being shot in the street. It was suggested to me that our media should ignore some things and vindicate others: in other words, propagate official ideology.'

But in Moscow — where 80 per cent of Russian money is concentrated — it is rumoured that in the days before the December attack, Most's banking competitors were tramping through General Korzhakov's office calling for 'something to be done' about their rival. And, not least, there is Gusinsky's long-standing link with Yury Luzhkov, the powerful and uncompromising mayor of Moscow, once a loyal supporter of Yeltsin's but now potentially a rival for the presidency.

Luzhkov used Most to handle the city's finances and helped its property companies to acquire some of the best sites in the capital. His relationship with Yeltsin has been bumpy in recent months. In March, following the gangland killing of the popular television commentator, Aleksandr Listyev, the president accused Luzhkov of being responsible for the spate of crime waves in the capital. Two of his deputies were dismissed and Luzhkov threatened to resign — a move that would have left him dangerously free to run in the presidential elections as a maverick hounded by the authorities. More recently the rift has been publicly patched up. Gusinsky's return to Moscow in May, timed to coincide with Luzhkov's public rehabilitation, is a reflection of the extent to which the fortunes of the two men may still be linked. 'Luzhkov is a kind of myth,' Gusinsky says. 'He's not a politician yet, though he may want to become one. An emergency could transform him.' The stability of the presidency rests largely with the mayor who controls much of the vote in the city: by undermining him Yeltsin would be shooting himself in the foot.

With parliamentary elections due at the end of the year and the increasing popularity of Gusinsky's NTV network, the Yeltsin camp evidently senses a threat to its monopoly of the airwaves. Ninety-nine per cent of Russian households own TV sets. Outside Moscow, television is the only source of entertainment for three generations of people living in apartments 35 metres square. Politically it is crucial. But for the government to attempt closure of NTV would be to invite embarrassing protest from the West. In December NTV carried harrowing war footage from Chechnya invoking memories of Vietnam. *Segodnya* hits out at the government almost daily. Both promote Gusinsky's underlying credo: 'Information empowers people to make choices. There are no other values in the world. There is the right to choose and the right to know about the possibility of choice. There is nothing else.'

On 1 April, Russia's state-owned nationwide television channel took to the air as Russian Public Television, funded now by a car dealer, an electronics retailer and six banks — all closely connected with the Kremlin, all reliably loyalist. The channel is expected to be a new presidential outlet, promoting the Kremlin's view in the run-up to the parliamentary elections in December this year and the presidential poll in July 1996. With a US$97 million injection from its new benefactors keeping the new channel afloat, bankers are becoming key players in the struggle for the hearts and minds of the electorate. There is a strong lobby in the business world to postpone both sets of elections for the sake of economic stability. A new patriotic bourgeoisie is acting as a watchdog for Russian interests. The Russian government has been offered a loan of US$1.65 billion by a group of banks — one of which at least has close links with the new, pro-Yeltsin group in Parliament, the anti-election 'Stability' — in exchange for state-held shares in some of the country's most coveted industries to protect them from foreign bidders. It's been dubbed the 'deal of the century', but Most has been excluded.

Politics and banking are high-risk occupations in Russia today. With the chasm between Russia's new rich and a new poor growing wider and contract killings up fivefold since 1992, 70 per cent of Russians now believe that law and order should be restored at whatever cost. In May, the Duma gave preliminary approval to a bill that would allow the Federal Security Services (FSB, a descendant of the former KGB) to engage in wire-tapping, monitor computer nets and set up files on Russian citizens. There is also talk of an increase in the security service budget. 'Something's bound to happen,' Gusinsky says. 'They've got to show how bad things are to justify their actions. Doubtless the 'mafia' will kidnap or kill a well-known western businessman. People are trying to protect themselves, remove potential rivals from the field or create a situation in which elections cannot take place. And the West, which is scared stiff of the Russian mafia, terrorists and fascists, will close its eyes to everything. Set your own house in order, they'll say. Basic freedoms will take second place. It's the American way and you can't blame them. American interests take priority. If these are favoured by dictators, they will get America's support. That's life.'

With a reported 16,000 additional army and Interior Ministry troops flooding the Russian capital in the wake of the Budyonnovsk hostage crisis, Gusinsky's fears may be well founded. The clamp-down — ostensibly against terrorism — put armoured personnel carriers on all main roads into the capital. A security alert can serve as the requisite excuse to impose measures that will ensure the unassailability of the ruling elite. Amid a fevered pitch of activity, the climate of fear affects everyone, particularly those with most to lose. And it is this, above all, that bonds the new plutocrats and Russia's political establishment. 'Every Russian leader knows that, if a new leader takes over, repressive measures may be taken against him, his family and his supporters. These are the vestiges of the martial mentality instilled in us by the Bolsheviks.

With Yeltsin rumoured to be consulting oracles and horoscopes, and the politicians at loggerheads, there can be little doubt where power in Russia really lies. And it is understandable why bankers are so reluctant to see elections undermine the cosy balance. 'Politicians have understood that they have to express the interests of financial groupings and not the other way around,' Gusinsky remarks. His own position on the wisdom of holding elections has been variously reported. But as we speak he insists that they must happen. 'To deprive people of the right to choose their government is to condemn everyone to far greater problems. If fair elections take place, if some television channels stay independent, then NTV will make its contribution. Provided the show goes on, and the actors are there and the lighting is in place and there are not machine-guns in the auditorium, we can play our part. There is no division of legislative and executive power in Russia today. Everything is concentrated in one pocket: that of the central authorities. Power isn't measured by the ability to impose it, but in the potential to exercise it. We are trying to encourage a division of power. But the image of a new, criminal power base is beginning to take shape here. It is rising up like the ghost in *Hamlet*. Once it is fully manifest, you can forget your Shakespeare. The play's over.' ❑

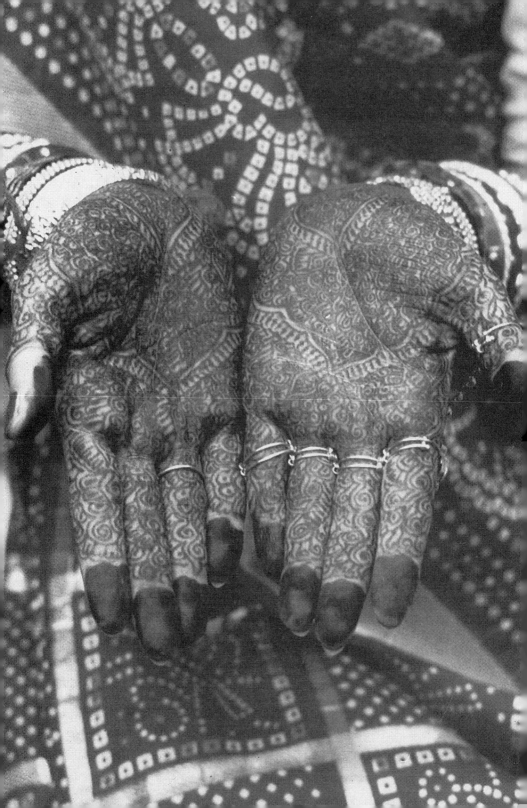

The body politic

As the world's women prepare to gather in Beijing, *Index* sets the missing agenda that will not be addressed

Left: Stefan Richter/Camera Press

NAILA KABEER

Selective rights, collective wrongs

Women, body-politics and the development agenda

Official development-speak calculates time in decades. The UN declared the 1960s the 'First Decade of Development', by which reckoning, we are now in the fourth decade of development. Women, however, were not discovered until half-way through the second decade: at International Women's Year in 1975. Which put 'Women in Development' just 20 years behind.

The reason the women in development calendar moves at a separate pace from that of the mainstream is the time it took— an extra decade and a half — to persuade policy makers and planners that women's specific needs and interests have been systematically left out of the development agenda. While this has been gradually rectified over the past two decades, the incorporation of women's issues into the development process has been on very selective terms.

Development interventions are primarily concerned with questions of production, investment and growth within the market-place, and human beings enter it as economic agents, bearing resources such as capital, education, entrepreneurship and labour. The concern of development planners is to ensure the efficient allocation of these resources; aside from the right to private property and the freedom to dispose of it, the rights of individual agents in the allocation process are none of their concern.

This extremely selective definition of rights within economic development discourse reflects the way in which economists think about the human agent. The economic agent has no body — it is an abstract, disembodied bearer of labour and other resources. The classic metaphor used to illustrate economic theories of production and exchange in economic textbooks was that of Robinson Crusoe: first on his own, deciding how to divide his time between production and leisure and then, with the addition of Man Friday, showing how exchange between economic agents occurred. The advantage of this metaphor is that both agents sprang into existence fully grown: the processes by which they were brought into the world, suckled and reared until they were capable of engaging in economic transactions, is of no concern to the economist and is conveniently excluded through this metaphorical device.

However, some of these 'non-economic' bodily processes have been the subject of attention from development policy makers and planners who cannot afford the ivory-tower abstractions of the academic economist. In particular, given that population growth rates in the Third World were identified very early on as a key constraint on economic growth, the need to intervene in reproductive processes has long been a major preoccupation for policy makers. If women figured at all in the early development agenda it was as overproducers of human beings. However, one of the major achievements of women-in-development advocates has been to persuade development agencies that investment in women is the key to the greater productivity of a nation's human resources. As one widely cited aphorism within the development community puts it: educate a man and you educate an individual; educate a woman and you educate the nation.

Women's claim on resources within the development process is thus premised on their role as instruments for achieving mainstream development goals. But development has done little to address women's rights as human beings, since the attention of development agencies is primarily on the relationship between individuals and markets. While women's human rights have been given some attention by other agencies concerned with these issues, here, too, the issue of rights is defined in a very selective way. This is exemplified in the latest report of Amnesty International.* Published to mark the Fourth World Conference on Women in Beijing this September, the report focuses specifically on the violation of women's human rights in China. It helps to highlight the category of rights violations which is deemed a legitimate area of public concern: the relationship between individual citizens and the state. However, its deafening silence on the violation of women's rights in what is deemed the private sphere of the family or the cultural traditions of society draws attention to the deep gender biases in the way in which human rights issues have traditionally been framed. ➤

BODY POLITICS

Authority everywhere tries to stamp itself on women's bodies.

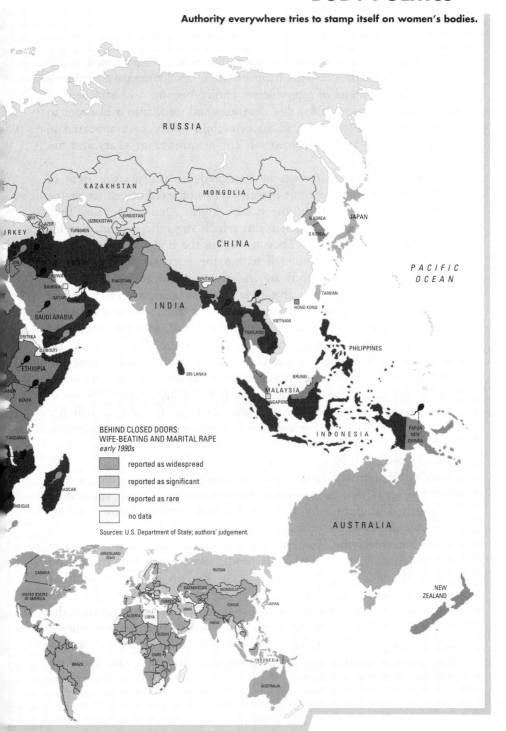

BEHIND CLOSED DOORS:
WIFE-BEATING AND MARITAL RAPE
early 1990s

- reported as widespread
- reported as significant
- reported as rare
- no data

Sources: U.S. Department of State; authors' judgement.

The main women-specific human rights violation mentioned in the Amnesty report relates to what happens when developmental attempts to intervene in the arena of reproductive choice become an instrument of state control. Reports of forcible abortions and sterilisations in order to ensure compliance with the state's one-child policy have appeared in newspapers and academic journals for a number of years and are confirmed by Amnesty.

As women's rights activists have argued forcefully, large areas of human rights violations are not perceived, or not acted on, either by the development community or the human rights agencies because they occur in the domestic/cultural realm which the official human rights agenda does not encompass. They also entail the body of the economic agent in a way that does not fall within the purview of development planning. Yet these violations are indivisible dimensions of the more visible economic inequalities that have found a legitimate place on the development agenda: in health, education, as members of the labour force and political participation. Until these unacknowledged violations of women's human rights become a matter for public concern, no amount of international conferences will succeed in challenging the bedrock on which gender inequality in the economic domain is founded. These violations represent assaults on women's bodily integrity and — in as much as the body is an essential dimension of the way in which a person experiences his or her selfhood — on women's sense of self-worth and selfhood.

While violations of women's rights over their own bodies may take culturally-differentiated forms, they universally subscribe to the view of women as lesser beings. A particular insight with universal application emerges out of Primo Levi's powerful and moving account of his experience in a Nazi concentration camp. It is easier, he argues, to deny a people's humanity when you have taken away their clothes, dressed them in identical uniforms, shaved their heads, taken away their names and reduced them to a homogeneous mass, known only by a number tattooed on their arms. Levi was writing about a unique episode in history, but his insights resonate with women's experiences all over the world. If there is one common factor in the way that gender inequality is maintained in different cultures, it is in the reduction of women to their bodies and the simultaneous construction of their bodies and, hence, of women themselves, as inferior.

We know — but do not know — about some of the more extreme forms of assault on women's bodies. We know, for instance, that women's feet were bound in pre-revolutionary China as a way of emphasising their fragility and vulnerability. However, it is unlikely that we would have known about the excruciating daily agony of hobbling around with bound feet if the writings of a woman like the author Jung Chang had not given us a detailed description of what it had meant to her grandmother. Jung's grandmother had no name; girls were often left unnamed in feudal China because they were considered so insignificant. Over three decades of socialist development has left China poised for superpower status but has not wiped out the age-old devaluation of women: instead, it has reconstituted it in a new form. While the Amnesty report details examples of abortions and sterilisations forced on young women, it does not touch upon the human rights violations in China visited upon its youngest female citizens. Alongside the official abortions demanded by the state are those undertaken secretly and voluntarily by women when they find out that they are carrying a female foetus. The number of boys born in China has far outstripped the number of girls, particularly after the first birth when the ratio of boys to girls shoots up. In addition, there are reports of infanticide as well as the large-scale abandonment of infant girls. Their fate in state-run orphanages was recently the subject of a UK television documentary which used hidden cameras to film what went on within some of these orphanages. It showed China's infant female citizens tied to chairs all day and left to survive as best they could. The names of many girl children in China today express their parents' desperation for a boy. But one little girl, who died soon after the making of the film, was called Mei Ming, which means 'No Name'.

Women who trespass on male space are considered to lay themselves open to sexual harassment and rape

Female infanticide is not unique to China. India has had a deficit of females in its population almost since censuses began. This deficit is largely concentrated in the north, where the cultural devaluation of females is much stronger; the southern states have traditionally had either egalitarian sex ratios or more females in the population than men, a

NAILA KABEER

Teheran, schools' exhibition: Iranian ambiguity

pattern that reflects female biological advantages in infancy and conforms to much of the rest of the world. Historical data tells us that there were whole villages in the north Indian state of Rajasthan where 'centuries had passed and no infant daughter had been known to smile within those walls.' Along with outright infanticide, the deficit of females in the northern states of India is also attributed to discriminatory feeding practices, denial of adequate health care to daughters and the pressure on women to bear children early, frequently and closely spaced in order to ensure sufficient surviving sons, that leads to high maternal mortality rates. The practice of *sati* — widow immolation — though outlawed, is also more widespread in the north; the most recent case occurred in Rajasthan.

Nor have several decades of development wiped out the cultural devaluation of women; rather the reverse has occurred with the deficit growing larger and now spreading to the southern states as well. A documentary by an NGO in Tamil Nadu, one of India's southern states where this reversal in number of females to males has been most rapid, records mothers relating the three most common ways in which infant girls are killed. Behind this reversal in south India is the adoption of high-caste practices, in particular the payment of dowry by a girl's parents to the groom at marriage, a process that has spread alongside increasing economic growth and the rise in female participation in the labour force. Also on the rise are 'dowry-deaths', the immolation of women by their husbands or in-laws because continuing dowry-related demands are not met. A recent analysis of excess female mortality found it to be highest in states considered the most economically advanced.

The other widely publicised example of violation of women's bodily integrity is female circumcision, widespread in parts of Africa. While men are also circumcised — an operation involving considerable pain — there are significant differences in the two operations. Henry Indangasi talks about the meaning of male circumcision among the Maragoli in Kenya as marking the transition from boyhood to manhood. Both surgery and healing are regarded as tests of courage and endurance for men so that they can 'walk tall' in the community. There is a ceremony, traditionally held six months after surgery, to mark the healing period. By this time there is no pain; and medical opinion suggests that circumcision tends to protect men from genital infection.

By contrast, the experience, the meaning and the aftermath of female circumcision is very different. Female circumcision varies from the milder version entailing removal of the skin of the clitoris with a fingernail performed in some communities on one-week-old baby girls, to more drastic measures: cliteridectomy or the removal of the entire clitoris; excision which is removal of the clitoris and the labia minora; and infibulation or the complete removal of clitoris and labia minora, and the stitching together of the walls of the vulva leaving only a small orifice for urine and menstruation. The beating and pain imposed on the young girl during the operation are intended to teach her respect and discipline; the knitting together of the walls of the vulva provide an extra safeguard of the girl's virginity. However, the pains associated with more drastic forms of female circumcision are not over after the healing period. Infibulation, in particular, destines women to a continuing cycle of pain, cutting and restitching to accommodate sexual penetration and childbirth. It can also cause health problems associated with retention of urine and menstrual blood, such as urinary tract infections, stones in the urethra or bladder, constant back and menstrual pain and repeated reproductive tract infections. In some cases, these infections lead to sterility. For women whose worth is defined in terms of their fertility, this can have devastating consequences. There are also severe psychological repercussions — depression, lethargy, fatigue and anxiety.

Rape as a form of violation against women has increasingly entered public awareness. Rape was long seen in popular perception as an individual aberration by men with uncontrollable sexual needs. Its roots in the cultural devaluation of women tended to be ignored or denied. Institutionalised gang-rape is, in fact, culturally sanctioned in parts of Papua New Guinea as a form of control over women. But its appearance as a weapon of war used to humiliate the enemy in a wide variety of contexts, is only now being recognised. Cases of the large-scale rape of women during war made known by the international media include the rape of Bangladeshi women by Pakistani soldiers during the 1971 War of Liberation; in Uganda, Rwanda and more recently in Bosnia. During the communal riots in India following the destruction of the Babri Masjid in Ayodhya in 1992 by Hindu fundamentalists, a video for illicit circulation showed the rape of Muslim women in Surat. It symbolised not so much the degradation of Muslim women, but the humiliation of the Muslim man who could not protect the honour of his women.

These are the more extreme forms of assaults on women's bodies and human rights that have forced themselves on public attention. However, there are other, more silent forms that are unlikely to figure in the media because they do not lend themselves to sensationalist treatment but are, nevertheless, a part of the process by which women's bodies are culturally defined as lesser, polluted or vulnerable. While births are welcomed in most of the world, the bodily processes entailed in reproduction are considered polluting by the world's major religions: menstruating women and the new mother and her baby are ritually cleansed before returning to normal life. In India, midwives are traditionally drawn from the 'untouchable' castes because of the polluting nature of the work. Women's bodies are also considered a source of temptation to men and, in Muslim and Hindu societies in particular, female propriety requires women to either remain secluded within the household or to veil themselves when they move around outside it. Women who trespass on male space are considered to lay themselves open to sexual harassment and rape.

Women's lesser status is also symbolised in the way that physical interaction with men is governed. Among some African communities, women must kneel before their husbands when serving them water; in Bangladesh, women keep their heads covered in public space to signify modesty. In Europe and the USA, violence against women often takes the appearance of choice. Eating disorders such as anorexia, or extreme weight loss induced by gradual self-starvation, and bulimia, binge eating followed by purging through vomiting or use of laxatives, is almost entirely confined to western industrial countries and Japan. The cultural obsession with the female body as sexual object, made pervasive by the powerful forces of the media, has also led to the practice of self-mutilation among women through cosmetic surgery, often with serious health implications.

The problem of domestic violence has no cultural nor class boundaries. In Britain, it has only recently been recognised as an arena for state intervention. In many countries, where women continue to be defined as the property of their husbands, domestic violence is seen to be a private matter. In cultures as diverse as Sri Lanka and Kenya, there are folk sayings interpreting wife-beating as an act of love.

Although these violations of women's human rights do not form part of the mainstream development agenda, their repercussions for many aspects of conventional development issues are receiving gradual recognition. The World Bank, for instance, has recently been able to bring out a report on violence against women by 'naming' it a health issue. Constraints on women's ability to move freely have been found to reduce the efficiency of the response to economic adjustment measures imposed by the IMF, in the name of economic growth, on a large number of low-income countries. An important cause of low female education in the Indian context has been found to be the lack of separate toilets for girls in primary schools. In Ghana, teenage pregnancies have long been a major reason for high rates of female drop-outs from school; family-planning services and information generally bypassed young unmarried women who were not perceived as sexually active.

In Rajasthan, Bhanwari Devi, a female development worker who had been campaigning in support of the government's ban on child marriage was raped in front of her husband by members of the upper caste in her village. Bhanwari Devi's case took over a year to reach the court and the fact that it did so was partly a result of the efforts of the Indian women's movement. In India, as elsewhere, rape brings more dishonour to the victim than to the perpetrator. In 1994, Bhanwari Devi received the

NAILA KABEER

Neerja Bhanot Award for her courage in standing up publicly to the most powerful members of her community. She has said that she will use some of her award money to build a toilet for girls in the village school. ❑

Naila Kabeer is a fellow at the Institute of Development Studies, University of Sussex. Her latest book, Reversed Reality (Verso, UK) was published this year

*Women in China: Imprisoned and Abused for Dissent *(Amnesty International, June 1995, 27pp)*
Body Politics text copyright © M Kidron & R Segal, 1995; maps and graphics coyright © Myriad Editions Limited, from The State of the World Atlas by M Kidron & R Segal (Penguin Books, £11.00), available from 7 September 1995

CHINA
The baby gulag

'Understaffed orphanages simply abandon baby girls who become ill and put them in a room and leave them to die.' For over a year, persistent but unconfirmed rumours have been circulating of the existence of dying rooms in China's state orphanages. Earlier this year, a UK film crew travelled to China to discover the truth. Posing as workers from a US orphanage and with cameras concealed in bags and suitcases, they criss-crossed five provinces and covered 4,000 miles to produce a documentary of terrifying sadness. The voices below, from the soundtrack, include those of a specialist in Asian demography, carers in orphanages, journalists, local officials and women who have been forced to abort their 'surplus' unborn children

'The one-child policy tended to not take traditional Chinese cultural preference for a son into consideration. Sons generally carry the family line, so obviously the son is more important than the daughter. Now that each family is limited to only one child, the gender becomes a very important concern to each family.'

'In this game of birth roulette you only get one chance to have a son. Peasant parents were put in a very difficult situation. If they allowed their little girl to live they wouldn't have a chance to have a little boy and so all of a sudden throughout China, even in rich areas, you began to hear reports of female infanticide, little girls are plunged into a bucket of water before they have a chance to draw the first breath.'

'At least 15 million baby girls have disappeared since the one-child policy began, that's two every minute. Many of them have been aborted once an ultrasound scan has confirmed they're female.'

'Girl babies are called "maggots in rice" in the countryside because their families have to pay to bring them up and as soon as they get into their teens they marry and leave their family to join their husbands.'

'With severe punishments for non-compliance [with government policy], many births are hidden from the authorities. This leads to many new-born babies being abandoned. Some of them maybe die of hunger. Some of them may be picked up by the gangs to become beggars in the street. And some of them may be lucky enough to be sent to an orphanage.'

Note from the government to orphanage: '13 February 1995, baby abandoned. No further information so we are now sending this baby here.' 'From now on she will be identified only by her luggage label. This gives her name, her approximate birth date and the day she was brought in. She is to be called Bao Ming, Ming meaning Brightness and Bao the surname given to all of this month's babies. Bao Ming is the tenth baby to arrive this month, if the month is to be average, another 25 are on their way.'

'They are little girls of course, unless they are *handicapped* boys, but healthy boys are never abandoned, ever.'

'We found toddlers tied to bamboo seats with their legs splayed over makeshift potties... She's got three pieces of string around her body, across her chest, across her middle and down by her feet...and then there's two layers of thick material in what's almost like a bodice around the body to keep her straight. And underneath it's very constricted, very tight, and she's very wet inside. It's another little girl.'

'They put a special medicine into the body to kill the baby. And when the baby's born they just throw it away. A woman is not important. She's just like a dress. If I like you today, I take you home. If I don't like you, I take you off and throw you away.'

'Unattended and bored, these infants spend their days tied together in a potty bench. With new-borns five to a cot in temperatures of over a hundred degrees — one in every five died. There was no time to separate the dying from the rest, this whole building is their dying room.'

'There was a room where a baby girl had been left to die 10 days ago. The staff preferred not to enter the room, waiting instead for one of the other children to report the infant dead. We asked her name and were told Mei Ming. This means no name. It was the second time in her short life she had been abandoned. Mei Ming gave up the fight for life four days after we filmed her. She died of neglect. When we telephoned, the orpanage denied she had ever existed.' ❑

> 'The pernicious practice of abandoning female infants has not been entirely stamped out in some remote rural areas, but it is rare.
> 'The welfare facilities in China provide orphans with adequate adopting, medical, rehabilitation and educational services until they reach adult age, when they are even helped with employment and marriage.
> 'The living conditions of orphans have been improving continuously.
> 'The so-called "dying rooms" do not exist in China at all. Our investigations show that those reports are vicious fabrications out of ulterior motives. The contemptible lie about China's welfare work cannot but arouse the indignation of the Chinese people.'
>
> *Summarised version of a Chinese Government statement, June 1995*

© Excerpted from 'The Dying Rooms', a programme made by Lauderdale Productions for Channel 4's Secret Asia series
For more information contact The Dying Rooms Trust, 68 Thames Road, London W4 3RE, UK

THE BODY POLITIC: CHINA

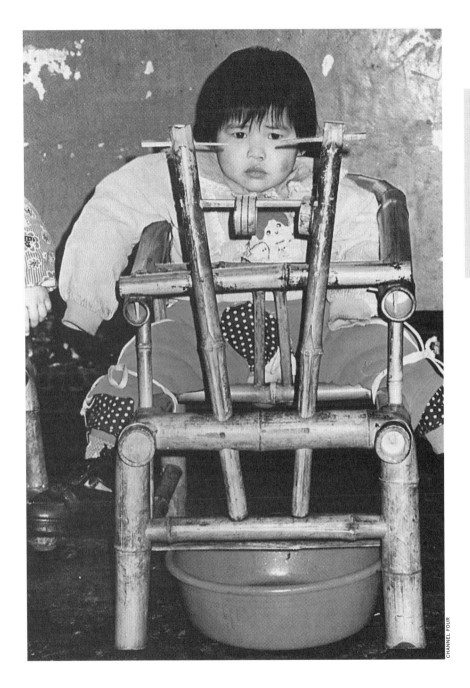

COVER STORY

ERICA JONG

Deliberately lewd

Pornography is to art as prudery is to the censors

Pornographic material has been present in the art and literature of every society in every historical period. What has changed from epoch to epoch — or even from one decade to another — is the ability of such material to flourish publicly and to be distributed legally.

After nearly 100 years of agitating for freedom to publish, we find that the enemies of freedom have multiplied, rather than diminished. They are Christians, Muslims, oppressive totalitarian regimes, even well-meaning social libertarians who happen to be feminists, teachers, school boards, librarians. This should not surprise us since, as Margaret Mead pointed out 40 years ago, the demand for state censorship is usually 'a response to the presence within the society of heterogeneous groups of people with differing standards and aspirations.' As our culture becomes more diverse, we can expect more calls for censorship rather than fewer.

Mark Twain's notorious *1601...Conversation As It Was By The Social Fireside, In The Time Of The Tudors* fascinates me because it demonstrates Mark Twain's passion for linguistic experiment and how allied it is with his compulsion toward 'deliberate lewdness'.

The phrase 'deliberate lewdness' is Vladimir Nabokov's. In a witty afterword to his ground-breaking 1955 novel *Lolita*, he links the urge to create pornography with 'the verve of a fine poet in a wanton mood' and regrets that 'in modern times the term "pornography" connotes mediocrity, commercialism and certain strict rules of narration.' In contemporary porn, Nabokov says, 'action has to be limited to the copulation of clichés.' Poetry is always out of the question. 'Style, structure, imagery should never distract the reader from his tepid lust.'

In choosing to write from the point of view of 'the Pepys of that day, the same being cup-bearer to Queen Elizabeth' in *1601*, Mark Twain was transporting himself to a world that existed before the invention of sexual hypocrisy. The Elizabethans were openly bawdy. They found bodily functions funny and sex arousing to the muse. Restoration wits and Augustan satirists had the same openness to bodily functions and the same respect for Eros. Only in the nineteenth century did prudery (and the threat of legal censure) begin to paralyse the author's hand. Shakespeare, Rochester and Pope were far more fettered *politically* than we are, but the fact was that they were not required to put condoms on their pens when the matter of sex arose. They were *pleased* to remind their readers of the essential messiness of the body. They followed a classical tradition that often expressed moral indignation through scatology. 'Oh Celia, Celia, Celia shits,' writes Swift, as if she were the first woman in history to do so. In his so-called 'unprintable poems', Swift is debunking the conventions of courtly love — as well as expressing his own deep misogyny — but he is doing so in a spirit that Catullus and Juvenal would have recognised. The satirist lashes the world to bring the world to its senses. It does the dance of the satyrs around our follies.

Obscenity is used in literature as a sort of wake-up call to the unconscious

Twain's scatology serves this purpose as well, but it is also a warm-up for his creative process, a sort of pump-priming. Stuck in the prudish nineteenth century, Mark Twain craved the freedom of the ancients. In championing 'deliberate lewdness' in *1601,* he bestowed the gift of freedom on himself.

Even more interesting is the fact that Mark Twain was writing *1601* during the very same summer (1876) that he was 'tearing along on a new book' — the first 16 chapters of a novel he then referred to as 'Huck

ERICA JONG

Finn's autobiograph'. This conjunction is hardly coincidental. *1601* and *Huckleberry Finn* have a great deal in common besides linguistic experimentation. According to Justin Kaplan, 'both were implicit rejections of the taboos and codes of polite society and both were experiments in using the vernacular as a literary medium.'

In order to find the true voice of a book, the author must be free to play without fear of reprisals. All writing blocks come from excessive self-judgement, the internalised voice of the critical parent telling the author's imagination that it is a dirty little boy or girl. 'Hah!' says the author, 'I will flaunt the voice of parental propriety and break free!' This is why pornographic spirit is *always* related to unhampered creativity. Artists are fascinated with filth because we know that in it everything human is born. Human beings emerge between piss and shit and so do novels and poems. Only by letting go of the inhibition that makes us bow to social propriety can we delve into the depths of the unconscious. We assert our freedom with pornographic play. If we are lucky, we keep that freedom long enough to create a masterpiece like *Huckleberry Finn*.

But the two compulsions are more than just related; they are causally intertwined.

When *Huckleberry Finn* was published in 1885, Louisa May Alcott put her finger on exactly what mattered about the novel even as she condemned it: 'If Mr Clemens cannot think of something better to tell our pure-minded lads and lasses, he had best stop writing for them.' What Alcott didn't know was that 'our pure-minded lads and lasses' aren't. But Mark Twain knew. It is not at all surprising that during that summer of high scatological spirits Twain should also

> Pornographic art is perceived as dangerous to political movements because, like the unconscious, it is not programmable. It is dangerous play whose outcome never can be predicted. Since dream is the speech of the unconscious, the artist who would create works of value must be fluent in speaking the language of dream. The pornographic has a direct connection to the unconscious

give birth to the irreverent voice of Huck. If *Little Women* fails to go as deep as Twain's masterpiece, it is precisely because of Alcott's concern with pure mindedness. Niceness is ever the enemy of art. If you worry about what the neighbours, critics, parents and supposedly pure-minded censors think, you will never create a work that defies the restrictions of the conscious mind and delves into the world of dreams.

The artist needs pornography as a way into the unconscious and history proves that if this licence is not granted, it will be stolen. Mark Twain had *1601* privately printed. Picasso kept pornographic notebooks that were only exhibited after his death.

1601 is deliberately lewd. It delights in stinking up the air of propriety. It delights in describing great thundergusts of farts which make great stenches and pricks which are stiff until cunts 'take ye stiffness out of them'. In the midst of all this ribaldry, the assembled company speaks of many things — poetry, theatre, art, politics. Twain knew that the muse flies on the wings of flatus, and he was having such a good time writing this Elizabethan pastiche that the humour shines through a hundred years and twenty later. I dare you to read *1601* without giggling and guffawing. ❏

> **If we ban whatever offends any group in our diverse society, we will soon have no art, no culture, no humour, no satire. Satire is by its nature offensive. So is much art and political discourse. The value of these expressions far outweighs their risk**

Erica Jong became internationally famous in 1973-4 with the publication of her novel Fear of Flying, *which sold over 10 million copies worldwide. She has also written several collections of poetry and six further novels, most recently* Any Woman's Blues

Excerpted from a paper delivered at a conference on Expression, Offence and Censorship, organised by the Institute for Public Policy Research in June 1995. A full report of the conference, including contributions from Bernard Williams, Michael Grade, Clare Short MP and Chris Smith MP will be published shortly. Details from IPPR, 30-32 Southampton Street, London WC2E 7RA, UK

GUSTAVE COURBET

Unveiling the origin of the world

After more than a century of seclusion, Courbet's The origin of the world *was unveiled in the Musée d'Orsay, Paris on 26 June. The model's identity has also been revealed for the first time: Jo, also known as the 'beautiful Irish girl' was J M Whistler's mistress. Commissioned in 1866 by Khalil Bey, one time Ottoman ambassador to St Petersburg, the picture hung, according to contemporary accounts by prurient visitors, well veiled, in his lavatory. Sold in 1868 when the Bey's collection was dispersed, the picture continued its clandestine voyage round Europe, re-emerging in Paris in 1955 in the possession of the analyst Jacques Lacan, still concealed behind a picture of more mundane aspect.*
At the Musée d'Orsay, it is displayed behind bullet-proof glass with an official in permanent attendance to monitor the reactions of visitors. The first day of viewing passed without incident JVH

LUDMILA PETRUSHEVSKAYA

Panya's poor heart

I HAD my child pretty late in life, and before the birth I spent a long time in the so-called pathology wing, along with other women who faced various complications; and actually it turned out I wasn't the oldest mother-to-be, there was one really elderly one, a woman of 47, everyone called her Auntie Panya and made slight fun of her, of her way of saying, pseudo-scientifically, 'I'm off to empty my bladder.' Auntie Panya was more or less illiterate, an unskilled worker with a wrinkled face and cunning, narrow little eyes, and she spent the whole time walking up and down the short corridor along the wards, waiting and waiting for her hour to come, as indeed all of us waited. But it turned out that she was waiting for something quite different from the rest of us, big-bellied, groaning women, many of whom had already been lying there motionless for seven months, just in order to give birth. Beneath the windows visitors shouted congratulations; our ward was on the first floor and we lay there listening to their shouts through the little open window. One woman my age had bad luck yet again for the umpteenth time; she was carted off and we all thought she might just make it this time, but that evening beneath the windows we heard a drunken cry: 'Cow, bitch, good-for-nothing... You've ruined my life, you rotten bitch, why did I ever get lumbered with you...' That was her miserable husband shouting, having found out, as all of us had, that once again she'd had a stillborn baby.

But anyway, Auntie Panya was a quite different kettle of fish and was waiting for something quite different from the rest of us. She walked about with her drooping stomach, waiting, as it later emerged, for them to give her — far gone as she was — an abortion on medical grounds; that was why she was there — and had been for some time. She explained that for the last six months her husband had been bedridden with back trouble, he'd been working as a carpenter on a construction site and had lifted something-or-other. They had three children, and she herself had had a heart attack the previous year and been granted invalid status, Category Two disabled, quite serious. We might all have exclaimed at her letting it drag on so long, but none of us did, because we knew that to begin with she'd been given a quite different diagnosis — a tumour, they said, but the tumour kept growing and growing, till finally it started moving around and jerking its little legs, whereupon Auntie Panya, having been led astray by the district and city health authorities, headed off with a whole pack of papers to seek justice at the hands of the Ministry in Moscow, and won her case, the stubborn woman, because with her heart condition she could really have died in childbirth and left her three children orphans. She spent a long time going from one department to another, her belly getting bigger all the time, and a good six months or thereabouts had gone by by the time she finally got put in this ward at the medical research institute, where all of us had come to await our fate.

Auntie Panya got given a good doctor, Volodya, who'd just saved the life of a baby that had been suffocating in its mother's womb, a little girl. He personally sucked out the mucus that had clogged up all the child's respiratory tubes, and two minutes after it was born the child let out a cry — these were the sort of legends that circulated about Volodya, and the mother of the little girl in question kept rushing up and down the corridors seeking him out, wanting to present him with an expensive lighter, but she never managed and was simply discharged. There was another legend too, that Volodya's own mother had died giving birth, and Volodya had sworn he'd become an obstetrician, and had thus fulfilled a genuine vocation. And all this contributed to the general puzzlement over Auntie Panya and the hostility towards her, entirely innocent though she was, for Volodya was in no hurry to give her an abortion, but kept coming to see her in the ward, measuring her blood-pressure, checking up on the various tests, while Auntie Panya kept waiting; and by this time it was already a human being, after all, that all these doctors were planning to kill, a human being in its seventh month, but Auntie Panya kept stubbornly waiting and didn't want to know anything about it; she'd had a directive from the ministry, and her children were waiting for her at home, along with her husband, unable to walk, in their cluttered little dug-out of a house on the construction site of a new electricity station. Auntie Panya worked on the construction site too, or rather, she was a watchwoman, an invalid; and ▶

what the whole family lived on God alone knows.

TIME passed, weeks went by, I finally got out of the pathology wing and migrated to the maternity ward, and at last my baby was placed in my arms, and it seemed that all my torments were over, when suddenly I developed a high fever and a boil came up on my elbow. I was dispatched forthwith across the courtyard to the infectious diseases department, setting off in winter weather with a pair of borrowed gumboots over my bare feet, three flannelette dressing-gowns over my nightie and a towel on my head, just like a convict, and behind me they carried my child wrapped up in a hospital blanket, for he too had got infected and had to be transferred. I walked along in floods of helpless tears and was led, feverish, into some pestilential barracks, and there separated from my baby, whom I'd already started to feed; and it's a well-known fact that once a mother's started to feed her baby, that's it, she's bound hand and foot to him forever, and you can't take the child away from her or she might very well die of it. These were the ties that bound me, walking along barefoot in my hospital boots, to the baby borne along behind me, wrapped from head to foot in a grey blanket; and beneath his coverings he uttered not a sound, didn't move, as if frozen stiff. In that pestilential barracks they swiftly bore him away, and now my torments carried on in a ward for people with infectious diseases, some with boils, some with fever, among them by this time Auntie Panya, empty, her contents by now removed. She was taking a vast array of drugs for both her heart and her blood infection, for she'd already had her abortion, they'd opened her stomach, but the scar had started to fester; apparently everything in that medical institute was infected. But Auntie Panya, the murderer, was now at death's door herself, she was struggling to pull through and the maternity hospital had been closed for repairs because of a terrible staphylococcus infection. The patients said that it should be burned down, burned, but that was just idle chatter.

I wept throughout those days, I needed to express my milk so that it wouldn't dry up, but my hands were infected, and they wouldn't allow us out into the corridor, so I couldn't wash. I was afraid of infecting my milk and asked at least for some spirit to wipe my hands, three times the nurse brought me some cotton wool swabs, but then stopped bothering, we can't waste all our spirit on your hands, she said. Auntie Panya listened in silence to me sobbing over my dirty hands, she had worries enough of her own to think about; she had a high fever which wouldn't come down, and finally Doctor Volodya, the murderer, came to see her. He put his hand on Panya's forehead, looked at her scar and suddenly ordered them to bring ice; Auntie Panya's milk had come for her dead baby, and that was the reason for her fever.

Finally my time was up, my torments were at an end, and after long discussion they brought me my baby, who after a week of separation had forgotten how to suck. Thin, pathetic, transparent, he was completely helpless, vainly opening and closing his mouth, and I wept over him while he cried.

Meanwhile that murderer, Auntie Panya, started getting up and walking about, holding onto the wall, because there was talk of her being discharged. She explained that she was in training, it was 12 kilometres on foot from her nearest station to the construction site; but they discharged her two days later, without bothering to go into these details, and she left, making her own way, as best she could, to the railway station.

And my baby gained strength, began sucking away eagerly, and within two days we were due to leave that pestilential barracks and go out into God's world, when suddenly a further event occurred. A new patient was brought in to the ward — with a high fever, undiagnosed. They brought her in and put her in that empty ward, where I was the only one still hanging around, waiting for my next meal. My new neighbour was coughing badly, she wouldn't answer my questions, and straight away I set off energetically to see the paediatric nurse in charge; I told her they mustn't bring the baby to a ward with a sick patient, and so on and so forth. Very well, they stopped bringing him in, but by this time I knew where he was kept, where his nursery was; I stood by the door where he was crying away. He was alone in the nursery, as I was alone in the ward; every ward had its corresponding nursery, and I knew now that this solitary wail was the wail of my hungry baby, and I stood outside the door.

And suddenly a kind nurse took pity on me, gave me a white gown, a cap and a gauze mask, and took me into the nursery to feed him. I sat in a corner and fed my darling baby, he calmed down straight away, and I started looking round the nursery. It was a clean little white room, divided into four sections with a cot in each, corresponding to the number of beds in the adult ward.

All the cots were empty — the new arrival with the fever had not yet given birth, but there was an incubator standing by the wall, a high-powered construction, covered in a transparent dome, and in the incubator a tiny baby lay quietly sleeping, squeezing up its little eyes just like a fully-grown baby. I fed my own one, I loved my own, but a fearful pity for this other little creature suddenly pierced my heart.

It was obviously a little girl, with its neat little ears and its peaceful, sweet little face the size of a small apple — boys are born rather coarse, I'd already seen enough to tell, and only little girls appear in the world looking so neat and refined.

I asked the nurse as she came in: 'Is it a girl?' — and she nodded and said tenderly, 'That little girl of ours is already drinking from the pipette.'

I returned to the ward, it was feeding time, and the following day I and my baby got out of that hospital for good, out into freedom. But one question torments me: wasn't it Auntie Panya's little girl lying there in the incubator? For that nursery belonged to our ward, and why had Doctor Volodya kept delaying with Auntie Panya, if not because this martyr of science had wanted to let the child reach seven months at least, until it was properly developed?

ALL these questions torment me, keep jamming up my head; over and over again I see poor Auntie Panya picking her way along the wall, in training to get herself home, and I keep seeing Doctor Volodya putting his hand on her forehead; but what worlds apart they seem, Auntie Panya and this creature, sleeping so peacefully under the dome of the incubator, wrapped in pink swaddling clothes, breathing so quietly with her eyes closed, and piercing every heart, except the poor heart of Auntie Panya, watchwoman and invalid. ❑

© **Ludmila Petrushevskaya** *is one of Russia's most prestigious contemporary writers and has recently gained international recognition through French, German and Italian translations of her work. A collection of her stories* Immortal Love, *appeared in Moscow in 1988 and is forthcoming in an English translation from Virago. The above story is from the collection* Po doroge boga Erosa *(The way of Eros), published by Russian PEN Books, Moscow, 1993*

© *Translated by Sally Laird*
Translation supported by funding from the Arts Council of England

Illustrated by Andrzej Klimowski

IRENA MARYNIAK

Made in Russia: Mary Kaye beauty reps

Beauty goes East

New world, new image. US beauty consultants head for
Moscow bearing a smile

Remember the *matryoshka*? That smooth, rotund, baffling, egg-shaped figurine, head swathed in a colourful kerchief, wooden torso strategically split to spill out any number of clones in regularly diminishing size? Traditionally, she was the embodiment of Russia's mythological vision of herself: Mother Russia, a self-perpetuating body expressing paradoxes of dismemberment and restoration, confinement and release. And she evoked too, that erstwhile ideal of Russian womanhood: reassuring, self-sufficient, fecund and indestructible.

But whither now? Relegated to souvenir shops or the far corner of the street kiosk, there is little about the *matryoshka* today that reflects either free-market Russia or the dazzling spectre of femininity it has spawned. Elongated limbs, six-inch stilettos, black Wonderbras and naked ladies strutting their stuff on ice floes or desert sands. They are all there selling advertising agencies and computers, or adorning the windshield where Stalin's image was once displayed. Health education posters warning against AIDS groan with shots of female flesh. And then there are the beauty contests: 'Miss Legs' (prize: video cassette recorder); 'Miss Bust' (prize: dual cassette player). Take your pick.

'As an elector, consumer and reader, I feel lost,' a Russian *Cosmo* neophyte confides, 'I'm not sure what kind of woman I should be. A thumping combination of blue-stocking, Joan of Arc, Carmelite nun and Marilyn Monroe? So I turn to *Cosmo*, and there I find an image of womanhood which impresses me with its spirituality, intelligence, understanding and tolerance. I want to try it — like a new dress — and begin the long journey to self-discovery.'

With *Cosmo* as the new Bible, Russian women are well on their way to conversion from a time-honoured aesthetic of virtue and redemption to a beauty cult sweetened with danger, eroticism and choice.

Culturally, Russia has been uncharacteristically coy about the female form. Women's bodies are seldom represented in Russian Orthodox religious art and, later, repressed by the radical intelligentsia in favour of socio-political ideals. In the 1950s a Leningrad publishing house refused to include a photograph of the Venus of Milo in a booklet about aesthetics on the grounds that it was pornographic. Official parlance declared Soviet society sexless and genderless. The Marxist emancipation integrated women into productive labour and guaranteed them political and civil rights, access to most trades and professions, and equal pay. 'Mama the Tractor Driver' may have had equal status at work plus monetary incentives to build up a family, but she was also expected to live up to a dual role as producer and reproducer.

Now the severe, grey-suited, collectively oriented, Soviet stereotype is out, along with the thick-set matriarchal ideal which complemented her. Western beauty icons have flooded the Russian market to galvanise consumer spending and summon a potentially awesomely influential sector of the population to heel. In television and cinema, rape and aggressive erotica are all the rage. Once Soviet celluloid-heroines symbolised the moral fortitude, courage and resilience of the mother country; today, Russian film critics say, the raped woman is an image of the totalitarian system ravaged by those she once held in bondage. And there is the hint, of course, that girls like it rough.

The sexual spectacle is one aspect of the new promotion and dissemination of womanhood as an aesthetic and marketable commodity. The flesh has been rehabilitated. The imported beauty myth promises women economic, professional and personal success, greater independence and moral well-being, self-discovery and self-fulfilment. It challenges their ability to take hold of their lives, their sexuality and their appearance, but only in exchange for perpetuating a new belief system and the multi-billion dollar industries that promote it. It is all there: the underlying message that femininity of itself demands improvement; the caste system in which models gain the status of the elect; the weight loss crusade; the purification rituals; the promise of grace and salvation through the spiritual mediation of the beauty product.

The contemporary positive heroine is often a two-headed hydra. Ideals of purity, motherhood and wisdom underpin images of the wanton seductress, unsteadily poised in the Russian porn market. The once derided image of the pretty, brainless woman associated with US commercialism has now become an object of yearning. Barbie has conquered, complemented by images of the ideal wife and mother, the family drudge — weak, dependent, predatory and tyrannical all at once.

Glamour has arrived to assault the tired and crumpled lives of women starved for decades of privacy, time and personal independence. Feminism was discredited by Soviet ideologues as bourgeois and a challenge to Soviet manhood and society. It threatened dangerously to erode traditional roles and personality traits. From the mid-1970s alarm bells were sounding in the Soviet press about the masculinisation of women, a weakening of their tender and nurturing qualities. In the popular imagination today, feminists are uniformly slovenly, raucous, vengeful, power-hungry, insecure and (most unforgivably) lesbian. 'Western feminists have teeth like sharks,' the writer Viktoria Tokareva has remarked. Power politics is widely viewed as corrupt by definition, and though independent women's groups are beginning to emerge, they are still too fragmented to constitute a movement.

Russian women have deeply internalised images long received through religion, folklore and ideology, all of which have conveyed that a

IRENA MARYNIAK

woman realises her essence only through motherhood; that domestic tasks are unfitting for men; that nature has exclusively endowed women with traits of nurturing, compliance, patience and sensitivity. There is little or no reassessment of entrenched gender roles and the concept of constructed identity is being heavily resisted. The lives of Russian women are cast to reinforce the stereotype: woman is self-sacrificing protector of authentic relationships in a corrupt world, bearing her biologically ordained burden, with the added gloss — now — of an inert pin-up-style beauty and sexuality.

Since 1988, beauty pageants have gained the status of a revered tradition in Russia and broadcast their award ceremonies to millions.

Russian Cosmo: 'a terrible beauty is born...'

Initially, the beauty contest was presented as a public-spirited institution to develop taste and self-confidence, and provide role models for work-a-day families. Today, they have become an unstable mixture of moral ideology and sexual intrusion. Success in the Miss Baltic Sea Contest, it was mysteriously suggested once, might help to improve the health of the maritime environment. Beauty will save the world. But to allay any niggling doubts, consider the daily scramble for food and feast your eyes on the prizes: fur coats; watches; make-up (for lipstick you can expect to pay the equivalent of a month's salary); recording and video equipment. Beauty is a route out of the poverty trap. Plastic surgery is available for the correction of aesthetic inadequacies and promises an improved emotional, sexual and professional lifestyle — breast enhancement appears to be most popular. Press reports dwell on the successful international careers of Russian models; foreigners advertise for skinny spouses in the press.

The beauty myth has crossed the steppes, but it has been complemented there by a re-accentuation of traditional images of motherhood. Professional women are photographed with their children. Childless and infertile women have failed to fulfil their most significant task in life: they are defective. Better be a single mother; better be socially powerless, exhausted, working double-time at home and work; better be a biologically ordained failure at work than a physiological oddity at home. Frustration and frenzy are preferable to ostracism, mockery or pity.

The unencumbered, slender ideal has made incursions into Russia only in the last two decades, in the wake of urban industrialisation and the attendant social and cultural mutations. Rural communities traditionally equated beauty with bulk (child-bearing hips, tough, hard-working, economically shrewd), and continued to do so long after educated sectors of the population succumbed to western stereotypes. The *matryoshka* is fighting hard for survival, and she may yet triumph over her effete and insipid western rival. A sexual toy has little lasting interest; a strong, productive, colourful beast of burden is more reassuring and — in hard times — a safer economic bet.

But meanwhile, if you plan to go west, girls, take a tip from the international beautician Mary Kaye. She has at least 8,000 reps in Russia now. Ask yourselves: how does your skin feel? Then show a leg. And smile, please. ❑

RUSSIA
No change on the home front

'A chicken isn't a bird and a woman isn't a human being,' goes the popular saying. The meaning couldn't be put more succinctly and its implications for Russian women are borne out by the country's latest crime figures. According to a recent crime report put out by the Ministry of the Interior on 19 June, 15,000 women — two per cent of the female population — have been killed by their husbands, partners or lovers. Another 14,000 have been raped.

Natalia Gaidarenko, a psychologist and director of the Moscow Centre for the Victims of Sexual Abuse, is quoted by Human Rights Watch* as saying that 'these figures in no way reflect reality. Ninety per cent of women who are raped don't report the crime.' She cites one of her patients who, on reporting her rape was told by the duty police officer, 'Find the rapist, get him to confess, produce a witness and then come back to see me.' Victims of domestic violence fare no better: they are confronted with the classic argument that this is a 'family matter' in which the authorities cannot get involved.

'After marriage, many women let themselves go physically and it's not at all unusual for their husbands to lose all interest in them,' says Evgeni Riabtsev, head of the public relations department in the Ministry of the Interior. She believes this explains the upsurge of marital violence in Russia. Marina Pisklakova, a doctor at the abuse centre, says that women whose husbands threaten to kill them and who look for help are frequently told, 'As long as you are alive there is nothing we can do for you...' Furthermore, according to research by an institute of sociology, 60 per cent of police officers who were questioned blamed 'the behaviour of the women' for domestic violence. Victim support centres that have recently been set up in towns thanks to volunteers, prefer to try to sort things out 'without recourse to the police'.

On 21 June, the Turkish nationalist daily *Turkïye* claimed, not without malice, to have discerned the reasons behind Russian *machismo*. 'Russia has lost control of its ethnic minorities; Russian men of their households. Hence all this aggression against their women.' ❏

Le Monde *25/26 June 1995 Translated by Judith Vidal-Hall*
* Neither Jobs Nor Justice: State Discrimination Against Women in Russia
(*Human Rights Watch Women's Rights Project, March 1995, 30pp*)

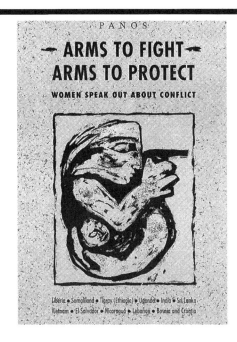

Moving personal testimonies from women fighters, active supporters of conflict, refugees and casualties of war, organisers for peace, and mothers, relatives and partners of the dead and disappeared.

These powerful, vivid, often harrowing accounts bring home the great diversity of women's experiences of and reactions to armed conflict.

"More than anything, this book does illustrate with stark personal records how greatly war affects development in general, but of women in particular."
Frances D'Souza, Article 19

"This book conveys women's sheer grit and determination to fight and to survive, and to bring to that survival a strength and dignity which surpasses the horror. Their harrowing experiences are all the more painful to comprehend because of the uncompromising, undramatic, unselfpitying manner in which they are told."
Helen Bamber, Medical Foundation for the Care of Victims of Torture

"This is a brilliantly researched and written book."
Glenys Kinnock MEP

Available from Panos, 9 White Lion Street, London N1 9PD Tel: 0171 278 1111
Fax: 0171 278 0345. Price £10.95, 288pp, maps, photographs, glossary, index.

CAROLINE MOOREHEAD

Bangladesh 1971: independent but still vulnerable?

Hostage to a male agenda

From Somalia to the Balkans, from Rwanda to Colombia, rape has become the ultimate weapon in the dying century's wars

Early in 1992, Maria Elena Moyano was elected deputy mayor of Villa El Salvador, a shanty town on the outskirts of Lima. She was 31, the mother of two young boys, and she was also the founder of one of Peru's most successful social movements, an association of women taking basic health services and education into the slums surrounding Peru's larger cities.

One evening, when she was addressing a meeting in Villa El Salvador, Maria Elena decided to speak up about the dangers of Sendero Luminoso, the Shining Path terrorist group which was reducing Peru to a state of permanent civil war. From the back of the hall, two men stood up and beckoned to her. Realising who they were, the audience began to panic. Maria Elena told them to stay where they were; the men, she said, had come only for her. As she walked towards them, they shot her. Her two sons were watching.

That spring, Maria Elena Moyano was the third woman leader in Peru to be killed within the space of a few months. Her death was particularly significant both because she represented the growing number of women activists — lawyers, teachers, human rights workers, politicians — who are now coming forward, and because it showed how very readily these women can be, and are, silenced. With the shooting, Sendero Luminoso delivered the message that the power and influence of grass-roots organisations among women, even those dealing only in health and literacy, would not be tolerated. In Peru's long-running war between Sendero Luminoso and the government security forces, women have been threatened, raped and murdered. Often, the same woman has been attacked by both sides.

Women are extremely vulnerable to violations of their basic rights, as the increasing violence of the 1990s is now making clear. Most of the world's refugees and casualties of war are women and children. And as repressive governments are discovering, women make excellent targets, to be killed, raped, ill-treated or taken hostage in order to humiliate and inflict pain on them, and because it brings pressure on their husbands and families.

In many parts of the world, women are now at constant risk from the security forces, simply because they are women. In *Making Women Talk*, Teresa Thornhill describes the treatment of a number of Palestinian women and girls picked up in the late 1980s in Israel and held as 'security detainees'. Under the Israeli military judicial system, investigations are almost always limited to interrogation with the aim of obtaining a confession. Most of the questioning is done by members of Shin Bet, the internal intelligence agency which, unlike the police, is not publicly accountable. Women who emerged after many weeks of solitary confinement talked to Teresa Thornhill of being deprived of sleep, food and even water, of being locked into boxes one metre square, of having revolting smelling hoods pulled down over their heads, and of being slapped and kicked. Then, after having been weakened by days of misery, they told of being tormented about the safety of their children, called 'whore' and threatened with sexual torture. For an Arab woman, sexual humiliation is shameful both for her and her male relatives, since men in traditional Palestinian society are seen as the guardians of female honour. One woman, who had been breastfeeding her child when the security forces came to arrest her, said that this was one of the worst moments of her life. 'I asked to be allowed to finish feeding him,' she said. 'This request was refused... This was the only thing that made me feel like...I am ready to die... I can still remember his crying.'

Nowhere, in fact, are the rights of women more comprehensively violated than by the legal process; and no country can boast that it treats its women as well as its men, or that all are equal in the eyes of the law. In Saudi Arabia in November 1990, a convoy of cars driven by women appeared in one of Riyadh's main streets. Police immediately arrested the drivers — Saudi women are traditionally forbidden to drive — and held them in detention until their male relatives had signed an undertaking that they would not drive again. Among the women were some who held excellent jobs. They lost them. A week later, the Saudi government passed a law formally prohibiting women from driving.

Nor are punishments and penalties everywhere the same for men and women. Dozens of women who were not wearing the obligatory *chador* were detained in Iran in June 1993 during a campaign against 'vice and social corruption'. Some were sentenced to be flogged, the penalty for infringing the dress code being 74 lashes. In Sudan, not long ago, women displaced by fighting in the south were given 40 lashes when it was discovered that they had been supporting their families by illicitly brewing and selling liquor. Two of them were pregnant at the time. In recent years in Bangladesh, local councils have set up *salish* courts of village elders, who have taken it upon themselves to pass sentence on girls and women accused of adultery. In January 1993, a young woman called Noorjahan Begum, whose first marriage had been dissolved, remarried. A *salish* court decided that it constituted adultery. Noorjahan's parents were flogged with 50 lashes, held responsible for her illegal second marriage. Noorjahan was buried up to her chest in the ground, then stoned. Some reports say that she died a few hours later; others that she survived, only to commit suicide.

Almost 50 years ago, the Geneva Conventions outlawed rape in war, 'Women', it declared, 'shall be especially protected...against rape, enforced prostitution, or any form of indecent assault.' Yet women, in almost every modern conflict, are being raped, both because rape is seen as a legitimate spoil of war, and because deliberate violence directed at women, and designed to dehumanise them, has become a recognised component of military strategy. Everywhere from Somalia to the Balkans, from Rwanda to Colombia, soldiers are being encouraged to become rapists.

Surprisingly little attention was paid to rape during modern wars, however, before reporters returning from Bosnia-Hercegovina revealed that the number of women being raped — in detention centres, refugee camps, prisons or even their own homes — had reached tens of thousands. Most of the victims were Muslim; most of the rapists Serbian soldiers. One 17-year-old Muslim girl, whose story is told in Amnesty International's *Human Rights are Women's Right*, was taken from her village to a hut in the woods in the early summer of 1992. She was held there, together with 23 other young women, for three months. During that time she was repeatedly raped. 'Rape', concluded the UN special rapporteur on the conflict in the former Yugoslavia recently, 'was...used as an instrument of ethnic cleansing...designed to terrorise the population and force ethnic groups to flee.' In Novi Grad, in June 1992, four Serbian women accused by their Croatian neighbours of giving shelter to Serbian fighters, were turned over to 15 men belonging to a group known as Fire Horses. For five hours, the women were gang-raped.

> Nowhere are the rights of women more comprehensively violated than by the legal process; no country treats its women as well as its men

It is not only during war that rape is considered an excellent tactic for control and repression, for the threat of rape, for many women, is the ultimate terror. Gurbetelli Erroz, a 29-year-old Turkish journalist working as editor for *Özgür Gündem*, a paper started in southeast Turkey to present the Kurdish cause sympathetically, has been repeatedly arrested for her supposed links with the banned Kurdish Workers Party. During one two-week period in detention, she was kept naked and continuously tortured. But it was not until she was threatened with rape that she signed a 'confession'. Rape, she said later, was for her the final and unacceptable torture. In Pakistan, human rights activists have told Amnesty International that they estimate that 85 per cent of the women taken into custody today are subjected to some kind of sexual abuse. Because to report rape can so easily turn into an accusation of illicit sexual intercourse, few women are willing to register complaints, particularly when the rape has been carried out by policemen or powerful local men. In October 1992, a young girl called Parveen from a village near Lahore in the province of Punjab was kidnapped and raped by four prominent local men. She was rescued, but the four men managed to get her rescuers arrested and then filed criminal cases against them. Parveen's father, who refused to be silenced, was shot dead.

The growing world population of refugees has brought in its wake not only terrible poverty, but endless stories of rape. More than 80 per cent of refugees are women and children. These women are particularly vulnerable to rape during flight from home, at borders and in camps. After some 300,000 Somalis crossed into Kenya in 1991 and 1992, many were raped in the camps in which they had sought shelter. There are reports of girls as young as four being raped. Elsewhere in Africa, a refugee woman escaping from the Mengistu government in Ethiopia was stopped by two men. She was five months pregnant. Describing the incident, she said: 'One pulled me aside and said "No safe passage before sex!"... He forced me down, kicked me in the stomach and raped me in front of my children.'

Women, however, appear to be fighting back. The noticeable growth in recent years of violence towards them has pushed many into taking a more assertive stand, encouraged by the determined women at the 1993 Vienna UN World Conference on Human Rights. Many have paid for their outspokenness with their lives. Women politicians, trade unionists and lawyers, all across South America, southeast Asia and Africa, have died in recent years while championing the rights of others. Some were working on behalf of 'disappeared' relations; others against torture or domestic violence; others again for land rights and indigenous people.

One singularly tenacious group of women has been the Tibetan nuns who have been beaten, tortured and sent to prison for shouting 'Free

Tibet' in the streets of Lhasa. Nearly a third of Tibet's hundreds of political prisoners are women, and most of these are young Buddhist nuns, like Phuntsog Nyidron, who had a nine-year sentence extended by a further eight years for recording pro-independence songs on a tape recorder smuggled into the prison. 'Our food is like pig food,' sung the nuns. 'We are beaten and treated brutally. But this will never change the Tibetan people's determination...' Another young nun, who managed to escape and make her way over the border to Dharamsala, told the magazine *China Rights Forum* that guards in prison had hit her face so hard that 'gradually I lost the sight in my left eye... They gave me electric shocks on my gums and lips.' Together with other imprisoned women, she was given the job of taking the excrement from the jail to a farm. They were given no soap, and later no water, with which to wash it off. 'Sometimes', she said, 'we sacrificed our morning tea to clean our hands.'

The Declaration of the UN World Conference at Vienna stated that 'The human rights of women and the girl-child are an inalienable, integral and indivisible part of universal human rights.' They are fine-sounding words, but it is hard to forget that, in many places, the lives of women still come cheap. According to a recent report put out by UNICEF, over a million newborn girls are murdered or left to die every year — simply because they are born females. ❑

Caroline Moorehead *is a writer and filmmaker specialising in human rights*

Further reading:
Teresa Thornhill Making Women Talk, *(Lawyers for Palestinian Human Rights)*
Human Rights are Women's Right *(Amnesty International)*
Untold Terror. Violence against Women in Peru's Armed Conflict *(Human Rights Watch/Americas/Women's Rights Project)*
News Review *(Tibet Information Network)*

Missing Women (over) *text copyright* © *M Kidron & R Segal, 1995; maps and graphics copyright* © *Myriad Editions Limited, from* The State of the World Atlas *by M Kidron & R Segal (Penguin Books, £11.00), available from 7 September 1995*

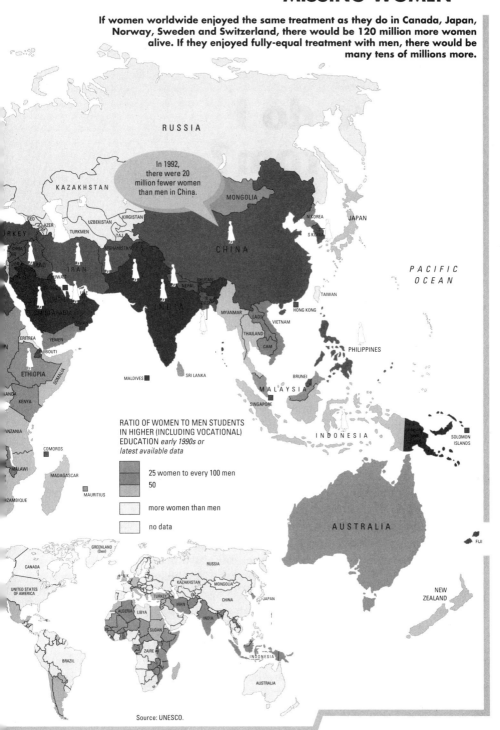

LEPA MLADJENOVIĆ

Where do I come from?

I come from a country where there is a war; in which all sides speak the same language and war rape usually means raping and killing women from the neighbourhood. One hundred thousand people dead, 10 times more injured. Five million people displaced.

In wartime the image of love, apart from being heterosexual, takes on an additional quest — to reproduce the nation. The image of sex, apart from being heterosexual and weighted with pornography, violence and Hollywood movies on TV, has an additional aspect — war rape. The women I speak to talk about being raped in private prisons, in barracks, in military warehouses, in concentration camps. Their homeless souls and courage haunt me in the nights; in the morning they provide the political framework for my work and strengthen my will.

In wartime, lesbian love has no language. Lesbians who are out must swallow their words; every word about their existence is seen as a desacralisation of the pain of war survivors. There is no such thing as an out lesbian in Serbia.

In Serbia, the nation-state rules. The range of possible identities has been reduced to a simplistic national formula: those who are faithful to the regime's policy of ethnic cleansing; those who betray it.

In Serbia, the regime creates a false reality: women's projects financed by foreign feminists deal with women abused by killers who come back from the front, but, says Serbia, it is not at war. It claims human rights are being protected when two million Albanians [in Kosovo] have no right to schooling nor the medical system and live in a state of siege; when thousands of gypsies live, as they have for years, in dark cellars and shanties; when half-a-million refugees are second-class citizens; when lesbians and gays do not have the benefits of marriage, are not safe at their workplace and live in constant fear. And when, if I want to work with women, I need to compromise with state institutions, knowing that in the Serbian Parliament and government there are men who are killers, rapists and war criminals.

When the war started, I came out on the streets to demonstrate my opposition to a murderous government. As the war went on, I felt the need to work with women war survivors. Supported by women from other countries, we feminists from Belgrade opened an Autonomous Women's Centre for women fleeing their families, male partners or the war zones.

Working in wartime presents us with a dilemma: how do we avoid the role men ascribe to us — to nurse the war-wounded? How do we interpret war torture when for some of us the world is gender divided? Should the heterosexual construction of roles force one gender into producing destruction and the other into sustaining that same destruction? I know many women feel the conflict between their roles as mothers and the demand for faith in the nation. But there is no social nor historic means to articulate that conflict. They plunge into deeper silence — the place they have known so long.

Feminist lesbians who live in countries afflicted by poverty and war must share my experiences. Trying and failing to understand why there must be war; surrounded by images of the dead conjured up by the blowing of the wind or an unexpected sound; with soldiers, proud of their killing, still wearing their uniforms on buses and in markets; while funerals become commonplace, and some of us are forced to conclude that some men like to kill. And this answers the question why.

Again supported by women from other countries, a few of us formed Women in Black against War. Every Wednesday we stand on the street to show our disagreement with the government. Some of us are harassed by the police as a reminder that 'they are watching us.'

There are no other peace demonstrations on the streets of Belgrade, only we who persist in believing that small acts of public disobedience are

> **The range of possible identities has been reduced to a simplistic national formula: those who are faithful to the regime's policy of ethnic cleansing; those who betray it**

meaningful. We know they don't change any political decisions but they change our lives and they matter to other women.

But I am not a war survivor, I am not a refugee, I am not a Serbian mother. The city I live in was not ruined. I am not identified with the regime, nor with the nation I come from. When the regime's newspapers call me 'a traitor to the Serbian nation' it touches off a secret smile.

I come not from the nation into which I was born, but from the lost lesbian country I never had and somehow still manage to create. If they cannot insult me at the national level they certainly can insult me as a woman and lesbian.

And they do.

When they hate you for who you are this is the beginning of war against you. I thought, if, tomorrow, pedestrians in the streets know I am a lesbian, how shall I hold my face together? How shall I open my eyes and not be affected by their disgust? How shall I not feel the same disgust about myself? Maybe the woman in the post office would want me to leave the post office immediately if she knew I was a lesbian? Maybe the woman on the market, if only she knew, would not sell me her strawberries? I felt so bad, I had to fight myself to restore my dignity, my passion and my politics.

Then I remembered the stories of women from the war zones and how they left their homes. Soldiers of different national colours would come to a village to be cleansed and order, 'Get out of your houses immediately.' Feeling humiliated but not knowing why, and with barely an hour to pack and run, and remember, maybe, to take a few photos, some coffee or an apple for the road. No warrant. I was cleansed in an instant.

But lesbians will remember. I know there were lesbians living in wartime before me. Most of them did not leave any guidelines. Women who loved women in my town a long time ago left no trace of their voices. ❏

Lepa Mladjenović *is a lesbian feminist peace activist in Belgrade and a founder of Arkadia, the Autonomous Women's Centre Against Sexual Violence. The above is excerpted from a speech made on receiving the Filipa de Souza international award in New York from the International Gay and Lesbian Human Rights Commission (IGLHRC) in 1994*

THE VOICE OF BRITISH FEMINISM

Everywoman magazine: covering the issues that matter every month

- **Yasmin Alhibai Brown** – Must we support women in high places?
- **The price of parenting** – Who should pay?
- **Ursula Owen** on the power of the word
- The politics of breast cancer
- Melissa Benn talks to **Barbara Follett** founder of Emily's list

PLUS ...
this autumn:
Women's Studies Supplement
The history of women's studies and full listings throughout the country

Every **woman**

£1.95 from major newsagents and bookshops or by subscription from:
9, St Albans Place,
London N1 ONX
Telephone: 0171 359 5496

On the line

Number of words in the English language for a sexually promiscuous female, 220, mostly derogatory; for a sexually promiscuous male, 20, mostly complimentary

Percentage of US female homicide victims killed by husband or partner: 33%

Percentage of senior positions in the UN held by women: 3%

2 million US women have received breast implants

8 million US women are enrolled in weight watchers

8 million US girls are sexually abused before 18 years

66% of women in developing countries have never been to school

66% of lower class female sex workers and 31% of high class sex workers in Kenya are HIV positive

69% of Bangladeshi women under 20 are married

44% of households in Barbados are headed by women

42% of used car dealers in New York City regularly charge women more than men

7,999 out of 8,000 foetuses aborted in a Bombay hospital in 1984 after prenatal sex determination were female

Pregnancy is the main reason for girls dropping out of school in the Caribbean

In Peru, 70% of all crimes reported to police are wife beatings

Police recorded 4,835 dowry deaths in India in 1990

65% of Columbian women declared that they had been hit by their husband or companion

Estimated value of female fragrance market by 1998: US$6.4 billion

Men outumber women 105 to 100 in Asia/Pacific: in the rest of the world women outnumber men

2 thirds of the world's illiterates are women

70% of children not enrolled in primary school are girls

89% of the world's parliamentarians are men

75% of the world's 18.5 million refugees and 20 million displaced persons are women and children

Algerian Olympic champion runner Hacibeh Bulmerka, has been condemned to death *in absentia* for showing her legs in public

Malnutrition among girls in Bangladesh is 14%, among boys 5%

Husbands in Botswana have a right to beat their wives for improper conduct

Women are 7 times more likely to be assaulted than men

THE BODY POLITIC: FACTS & FIGURES

Chinese police handled 15,000 cases of the sale of women and children in 1993
70% of respondents to a Chinese survey agreed that 'a woman's virginity
is more important than her life'
Backstreet abortions in Guatamala kill 3-5 women a day
200,000 Nepali girls are owned by brothels
Women receive only 51% of male wages
Jordanian husbands have the right to discipline wives; wives need husband's
consent to obtain a passport
On average, Russian women have up to 8 abortions
during their reproductive life
18% of Russian population have access to birth control
50% of Russian condoms rupture on first use
10 times more Russian women die delivering children than in
other developed countries
Nearly every Tutsi woman who survived the massacres in Rwanda was raped;
2,000-5,000 women conceived through rape
A woman is 10 times more likely to be raped than to die in a car crash
A woman over 65 has a 60% greater chance of living in poverty
than a man of the same age
Black women are nearly 4 times as likely to be murdered as white women
70,000 women have registered claims against silicone-gel breast implant
manufacturers; proposed settlement of lawsuit is US$4.2 billion
A woman is battered every 15 seconds
21% of married women report physical abuse by their husbands
1.5 million women are assaulted by their partner every year
In Thailand 200,000-400,000 girls under 16 earn money by selling sex
90% of women in Canada's mental health system and 80% of women in prison
were sexually or physically abused as children
Only 29% of white high school girls in the USA are 'happy the way I am',
compared to 46% of boys
30% of girls in India were breastfed compared to 51% of boys
In the Kallar community in Madurai, South India 51% of families questioned
admitted to killing a girl baby within a week of birth
90 million girls who are alive today have endured genital mutilation

Compiled by Laura Bruni and Nevine Mabro
Sources on page 112

EMMANUEL WOTANY

Thou shalt not suffer a witch

Times are hard in Burkina Faso and the young vent their frustration on the old and defenceless

Witchcraft in Africa is as old as the world itself. Contemporaries claim it as the traditional African religion, more often benign than malign in its practices.

With the advent of Christianity and Islam, most Africans discarded the old religion, but in one West African country at least, a revival of the practise has put the subject on the parliamentary agenda and forced the Catholic Church to set up refuges for women driven out of home and community by accusations of witchcraft.

The past decade in Burkina Faso has seen at least 600 women, all in their mid-60s, banished from their communities, often by close relatives, for allegedly murdering or causing a variety of other offences. The 'victims' of such misfortunes believe themselves cursed by the evil eye. Most of the women who have found shelter in the centre run by a Catholic mission in Burkina Faso's capital, Ouagadougou, claim they have been made scapegoats for the worsening ills — deepening poverty, joblessness, lack of opportunity — in their society. Many were leaders in their community, organisers of women's groups and mediators on issues concerning women. Cut off from their work and influence in the politics of their villages, they lead a solitary, twilight life with friends and relations for the most part too scared to visit them.

'All the women you see here have been banished either by their relatives or their communities for allegedly bewitching somebody in their villages,' says sister Marie Louise, the nun in charge of the Zwedu centre, adding that the centre was founded in response to the growing number of elderly women flocking to the mission with their tales. 'Some arrived

THE BODY POLITIC: BURKINA FASO

Catholic mission, Ouagadougou, Burkina Faso

here with scars on their bodies from beatings inflicted by angry members of their villages.'

Such is the tale of 68-year-old Cecila Yameogo, expelled by her own children following the death of her granddaughter, whom she was accused of bewitching, eight years ago. 'It was around 2am in the morning that I was ordered by my eldest son to leave the house and village or he matchete me to death,' said Mrs Yameogo with tears running down her cheeks. 'What can the rest of the family do against him,' she asks, 'when they were a party to the decision? Even my husband was helpless. His son had consulted the village witch doctors. They said I was responsible for the death of my granddaughter.'

With nowhere to go, she continued, 'I spent the rest of the morning on the doorstep of a local primary school and at dawn I walked nearly 100 kilometres for five days without food or money to Ouagadougou to my junior brother.' This brother, she said, 'refused to receive me because he had already heard from the village that I am a witch.

'It was then I decided, without any knowledge of the existence of this centre, that as a Catholic Christian I must go to the Ouagadougou cathedral to explain my plight to the priest.' At the mission premises she 'was surprised to learn that all these other women are also here for the same reason'.

'Since I arrived here, none of my relatives (husband and son) or children have dared visit me or send a word. At times I wish I should be dead rather than living, going through all this at a time in my life when I should be pampered by those I took care of in their teens. I don't deserve such treatment after all that I have done for these children,' she weeps. Even those who die in the centre, says sister Marie Louise, are buried without any of their relatives at the burial ceremonies. 'We always try to locate and inform their families. But no-one ever turns up. They only send us letters, expressing their happiness that their relatives are dead.'

Michel Nana, a member of Parliament and sympathetic to the women's situation, tabled a motion in Parliament this year, alerting fellow MPs to the problem in the hope of getting a law against the practice passed to protect the women. His efforts did not go down well with his colleagues, most of whom, he says, 'are staunch believers in the existence of such a practice'. 'There are no means of proving someone has hexed another,' says Nana, 'and that's why only the old and helpless, particularly women, are always the victims of the accusations.'

Justine Traore, another resident at the centre accused of killing her 'prosperous sister out of jealousy', said the method used in her village to prove that one has bewitched another is highly questionable. In her case, the body of her deceased sister was carried in a procession by four people believed to be vested with special powers, directly to her house. 'That is how they do it and automatically accuse you of killing, saying it is the body that directs and controls them to the killer's house.' She asks, 'Could you imagine that I would kill my sister who has been taking care of me? For what reasons?'

More often than not, she says, it is the younger generation who want to eliminate the old ones, thinking they are responsible for their own lack of success in life. 'Sometimes it is out of hatred', Mrs Traore said.

But are they really witches? 'Not at all! How can you imagine that a women who has suffered with nine months pregnancy for a child, toiled to bring her up, will kill the child?' a woman demanded.

Government efforts to stamp out the practice have failed. 'The average Burkinabe strongly believes in witchcraft,' claimed a Catholic priest. Teams of local workers sent through the towns with bullhorns, pamphlets and pictures designed to discourage people from expelling their old women were frequently driven out, often violently, and the government hastily abandoned the scheme. ❑

Emmanuel Wotany is Cote d'Ivoire correspondent for the BBC African Service

URVASHI BUTALIA

Hidden histories

The history of the bloodstained partition of India in 1947 is well known: 12 million displaced, over one million dead. The story of tens of thousands of women killed 'for the honour of their community', abducted, raped, abandoned, has yet to be told

In 1947 India freed itself from colonial rule and became independent. The euphoria of independence was overshadowed by another event, the partition of India into two countries: India and Pakistan. Throughout the struggle for freedom, nationalists had imaged the country in feminine terms: India was the motherland. When another nation — Pakistan — was carved out of its territory, it was as if the body of the mother — India — had been violated.

Partition also meant the dislocation of millions of people: estimates put the figure as high as 10 or 12 million, with Hindus moving from Pakistan to India, and Muslims from India to Pakistan. This mass movement on foot, by train, bus, cart was marked by unprecedented violence as members of each community killed, looted and violated the other. Women were particularly targeted: in both religious communities, women were killed, or made to commit suicide, by members of their community in order to 'protect their honour', something that became synonymous with the honour of the community. The fear was that if captured by the Other, women would be forced to convert, or have sexual congress with the Other, thus diluting the 'pure' race.

Thousands of women were captured, abducted, raped by members of the other community. The figures range between 33,000-50,000 Hindu and Sikh women and 21,000 or so Muslim women. In an attempt to recover their 'property', both newly-formed nation-states agreed to mount a 'rescue' operation in which women who had been abducted, or indeed those who might have gone of their own accord, were hunted out and forced to come back to their 'home' — regardless of their wishes. The women — particularly on the Indian side — had no choice. On the Indian side, this operation lasted until 1957; by this time many 'abducted' women had had children, and they were forced to undergo a second dislocation. Often, having been thus polluted, their families would not take them back. If women had children, they were even less welcome in Hindu families as children were 'living symbols' of impurity. So, they had to either give them up (usually to orphanages) or have forced abortions if they were pregnant.

The fate of these women was the subject of intense parliamentary debate in the course of which the woman's body became synonymous with the body of the nation: though the nation was now truncated, the woman's body, 'polluted' against her will, had to be recovered and repurified.

Much of what ordinary people went through in partition — the underside of the history of this event — is retained in collective memory. Partition stories form the staple on which many post-independence first-generation children were brought up. On the rape and violation of women's bodies and their abduction, however, there is a resounding silence. No-one speaks of it. If they do, they will indicate it happened to 'someone else', as if by being abducted and raped, the women themselves were somehow to blame.

I first learnt about this hidden history from a social worker who had worked with abducted women. While 'official' history provides some clues to what the state had to say on this subject, it was the silences in people's speech that gave an indication of how deep this particular trauma had gone. Eventually, I managed to track down some accounts of what women had suffered through memoirs written by women social workers and through interviews with them.

While several of the women who had been raped and abducted and subsequently 'rescued' are still alive, they will not speak about this experience; often, it is unknown to their families. The only access we have to their experiences is through the voices of social workers like that below. Women held back from speaking about their experiences for more than two decades because they felt it would be too painful to break the silence. Eventually, they did.

But first, the following account by a young man of the killing, by his father, of his sister in order to save the 'honour of the community'. The story is from the village of Thoa Khalsa in Rawalpindi (Pakistan), where about 100 women threw themselves into a well to 'save their honour'. Three of them did not die. There was not enough water in the well to drown them all.

'In Gulab Singh's *haveli* [house] 26 girls had been put aside. First of all my father, Sant Raja Singh, when he brought his daughter, he brought her into the courtyard to kill her, first of all he prayed...saying, "*Sacche badshah* [true god], we have not allowed your Sikhi to get stained, and in order to save it we are going to sacrifice our daughters, make them martyrs, please forgive us..."

'Maan Kaur, my sister came and sat in front of my father, and I stood there, right next to my father, clutching on to his *kurta* as children do, I was clinging to him...but when my father swung the *kirpan* [Sikh sword, emblem of the faith] perhaps some doubt or fear came into his mind, or perhaps the *kirpan* got stuck in her *dupatta* [veil, scarf]...no-one can say...it was such a frightening, such a fearful scene. Then my sister, with her own hands moved her *dupatta* aside and then he swung the *kirpan* and her head and neck rolled off and fell...there...far away. I crept downstairs, weeping, sobbing and all the while I could hear the regular swing and hit of the *kirpans*.'

In my research I came across many such accounts. Today, in remembrance rituals all over north India, the 'brave women' who 'voluntarily' gave up their lives are remembered and talked about. No-one speaks of the abducted and raped woman. This is why the following accounts are so rare.

Urvashi Butalia *is a founder of the publishing house Kali for Women, Delhi*

The following excerpts are taken from Mool Sota Ukhdela *(Torn along with roots) by Kamalaben Patel. Published in Bombay in Gujarati, 1982. This translation by Svati Joshi*

Ismat's story

Before partition, an aristocratic family of Rawalpindi [now Pakistan] used to go to Kashmir every year to spend their holidays. Similarly, a Lalaji's family from Amritsar [now India] also used to go to Kashmir. Both families stayed in the same hotel and met quite often, so naturally the elders and the children of the families became friendly. This continued till partition.

One of the sons of the Lalaji was called Jitu and the middle daughter of the Pathan family was called Ismat. The friendship between 14-year-old Ismat and 17-year-old Jitu developed into something more delicate...but it was not until partition, when Ismat was faced with the thought of never being able to meet Jitu again, that she realised what she really felt for Jitu, and she became very restless.

The only thing she knew was that Jitu's family lived in Amritsar...she started to think of ways to reach Amritsar to meet Jitu at any cost...and left at about eight at night for a Hindu refugee camp a mile away.

It was hardly a month after partition. The Hindu refugee camp used to be overcrowded. Several trains used to run to reach the Hindu refugees to Amritsar in time. The Indian army was in charge of managing this camp. Ismat went straight to the army commander of the camp and told him with great courage, 'I am a Hindu girl. I have been separated from my parents. Please send me to India immediately.' The commander was aware of the danger of keeping a young girl like her in the camp. He took her to the Rawalpindi station in his own jeep and put her on a refugee train ready to leave for Amritsar...

The Hindus and Muslims spoke the same language in Punjab, their manners were similar and their way of dressing was also similar. So there was no reason to suspect that Ismat was not a Hindu... During her talks with the workers of the camp she was able to get Jitu's address in about four days and also managed to send him a message to meet her at the camp. Immediately Jitu came to receive her. People who heard them talk to each other began to suspect that she was not a Hindu. Also, she was under-age, so they did not let her go with Jitu...

Jitu and his parents took the necessary permission from the district commissioner to take Ismat with them so the manager of the camp handed her over to them. Before our volunteers could obtain a stay order, Jitu and Ismat were married in the Golden Temple of Amritsar. Jitu's family gave consent to the marriage and they began living happily.

[Then] the agreement for the reclamation of abducted women was signed between India and Pakistan. At a meeting of the ministers of the two countries the Pakistani minister for rehabilitation himself requested the Indian minister Gopalswami Iyengar to return Ismat to Pakistan. Iyengar promised to make the necessary enquiries.

This matter was discussed in the Search Service Bureau of Amritsar which was concerned with the search for refugees and it even reached Jitu. He told me the entire story from the beginning and very firmly said that this was not at all a case of abduction. He asked me to help him. I told Jitu that their case had become a case between the two countries, that is, at an international level. Therefore I was not in a position to say anything with certainty about whether I would be able to help him or not.

This case was discussed at another meeting of the state-level officers in Lahore... I told Punjabi [an official], 'How can the case of a girl who has herself taken such a risk be considered that of abduction? Besides, how can the Indian government send her to Pakistan against her will?'

Mr Punjabi said in reply, 'How can the parents of a 14-year-old girl be convinced with this argument? Would not even we try to get back our own 14-year-old daughter who had run away, at any cost? Until we send Ismat to her parents the Pakistan government will never be ready to sign an agreement to recover abducted Hindu women from the northwest region of the border. Instead of giving importance to individual feelings we should think only of the larger community of people.'...

The pressure from Pakistan for this case continued. Later, a rumour was floated that Ismat's case was cleared and that Pakistan had agreed to let Ismat remain in India. The purpose behind this rumour was to convey this news to Jitu and Ismat. In a few days both were back in Amritsar.

An uncle of Ismat worked in the department of foreign affairs in the Pakistan government. We requested him to come to Delhi and discuss the whole matter. When he was in Delhi a meeting between him and Ismat was arranged. It took us nearly four to six days to persuade Ismat to go with him, meet her parents and then come back...

After great effort Ismat agreed to go on condition that Jitu would accompany her. When the details were worked out they left for Amritsar immediately by an afternoon flight from Delhi. I went to receive them in Amritsar with a car from Lahore. Jitu of course had no doubt about what decision Ismat would take...

On reaching Lahore we went to the Pakistan Secretariat where we were supposed to hand over Ismat to the inspector general of police. Ismat continued to sit in the car and was willing to go only if Jitu went with her... Finally Jitu himself talked to her and sent her to Khan Saheb's house with Mr Razvi and her uncle with a promise that he would meet her on the seventh day...

It was dangerous for Jitu to stay in Lahore for seven days. So the next day we dispatched him to Amritsar asking him to return on the seventh day. Reluctantly, he left for Amritsar.

When we inquired at Khan Saheb's we were told that [Ismat] had gone to stay at her father's house. We got the address and Mridulaben and I went there. The news of our arrival was sent to the women's quarter. After some time her father came. His behaviour was rude. After great hesitation he called Ismat. When we saw her we thought for a moment that the person was not Ismat but her sister. Her dress, her manners, even the expression on her face — all had changed. She pointed to Mridulaben and said to her mother, 'Amma, this is the short-haired woman who was stopping me from coming here. I asked her several times to bring me here but she used to avoid it.' ... As if waking up from a nightmare I composed myself with great effort and asked Ismat, 'When we parted at the secretariat you had promised in Jitu's presence to tell us your decision. What do you wish to do?'

She jumped at the name of Jitu and roared at us, 'I do not wish to see the face of that son of a kaffir. If I could, I would tear him to bits and throw the pieces to a dog.' There was no reason for us to stay there any longer...

When Jitu stood before me three days later I was extremely distressed to see his worn-out and sad face. His anger knew no bounds: 'You have all betrayed me. Nina (Ismat) had promised in my presence that she would announce her decision and today was fixed for it. You take me to her. I want to hear her decision from her alone. I don't trust any one of you now.' I tried hard to explain things to him but he would not be pacified. I called the officer who had mediated in this case to arrange a meeting between Jitu and Ismat if only to assure him. That bureaucrat coolly replied, 'Those people have left Lahore. If you wish to accept my advice then see that this boy doesn't come to Lahore. Now there is no safety for him here.'

But Jitu was not ready to listen to anything I said. He said: 'Even if she said this under pressure from her parents she would have changed on seeing me. You should have taken me to her. Why did you go alone?'... I tried very hard to make him realise that there was danger for him in Lahore. He was not prepared to hear any of this. He said, 'I am ruined already. Where is the harm in dying now?'...

I met him on the Frontier Mail when I was going to Bombay from Delhi in 1952. His face was very pale and he had grown very thin. The person travelling with him told me that he had TB and the doctor had advised him complete rest. But he neglected the doctor's advice and went where he liked and did what he liked.

I had no heart to say a few words of advice to him.

Veera's tale

We received a petition to recover a man's daughter from the police sub-inspector of a village in Multan district [Pakistani Punjab]. All the facts regarding her name and address were correct so our district woman worker went to see her. The daughter said: 'My father has given his consent to my marriage and I do not wish to go back to India.' We informed the father. In reply he said: 'My daughter has been forcibly taken away.' Whom were we to believe?...

I insisted that she should be brought to the Lahore camp to find out for sure whether she was refusing to go to India under pressure, and then after some days, to present her before the tribunal. If a Hindu woman was kept in a police officer's own house forcibly then what kind of a job would the police do to reclaim other women? She must be brought to the Lahore camp to set an example...

Finally Veera was brought to our camp. The moment she entered she shouted at the superintendent: 'Aren't you ashamed of forcibly bringing a married woman? I want to stay with my husband. I have nothing to do with my parents.' Immediately the police called and said: 'You finish talking to Veera then we will come to fetch her.' Once a woman was in the camp, the Pakistani police couldn't take her away by force and there was still some time before the tribunal was to meet. But her rebellious eyes, her lips pursed with determination and her firm attitude made it difficult to figure out the truth.

One night when I was ready to go to bed, the superintendent brought Veera. I asked her to sit on my bed and gently stroked her back. She broke down. When she had quietened down, she began to talk. She asked me: 'Women in the camp say there is a lady with short hair dressed in Punjabi clothes who can do anything in India. Even Pandit Nehru has to listen to her. If I tell the truth, will she listen to me?' I said, 'Certainly'. Here is the gist of Veera's narrative:

The families of the sub-inspector and Veera were good neighbours. During the riots the sub-inspector told Veera's father that if he married his daughter to him, he would reach the rest of them safely to the Indian border. Helpless, the father decided to save everybody's lives at the cost of his daughter's and got them [the sub-inspector and his daughter] married. He gave them 30 *tolas* of gold and the house they were living in. When the reclamation of women began, he applied to recover his daughter. The sub-inspector had a wife and children. Of course, he used to keep Veera well but when he was out, his wife used to treat her like a servant and called her a kaffir's daughter.

Veera had begun to detest her parents as they had sought her brothers' and their own safety at her cost. And it was for this reason that she decided to suffer but not to return to her parents. I promised her that we would do as she wished and would not send her back to her parents. If she wished to marry we would find a suitable young man and get her married. But she would have to disclose these facts before the tribunal. For the Pakistani police this case had become a prestige issue.

Veera's case came up before the tribunal. Mr Razvi said that the accused belonged to his own department and he wished to be present during the case... Veera said that she was willing to go to India and her marriage had been performed against her wishes. There was such anger and murder in the police inspector's eyes that he would have shot both Veera and me there and then if he could. When Veera demanded her 30 *tolas* of gold he said baseless things in reply. I told Veera, 'You can expect kindness from human beings, not from animals. God will give you everything. It does not behove us to ask him for anything.'

After some time, we found a nice young man for Veera and got her married. After years, when I met her in Delhi quite by chance, she was a mother of two children, and happy... ❏

FEMINISTS FOR FREE EXPRESSION

> To suppress free speech in the name of protecting women is dangerous and wrong. — Betty Friedan

Feminists for Free Expression (FFE) is a not-for profit organization of feminists fighting censorship in North America.

FFE believes freedom of expression is especially important for women's rights. Book, movie and music banning diverts attention away from the substantive causes of social ills such as sexism and violence against women. Censorship has traditionally been used to silence women and stifle feminist social change. It has never solved social problems.

FFE ♦ provides a leading voice opposing state and national legislation that threatens freedom of speech and the First Amendment ♦ defends the right to free expression in court cases, including those before the U.S. Supreme Court ♦ supports the rights of artists whose work has been suppressed or censored ♦ provides expert speakers to universities, law schools and the media throughout the United States and Canada.

For additional information about FFE, to join, or to contact our Speakers Network, please contact:

Feminists for Free Expression
2525 Times Square Station
New York, New York 10108, USA
Phone 212-702-6292, Fax 212-702-6277
e-mail: ffe@aol.com

NICARAGUA

The wheel of power and control

'What's happened to our reproductive and sexual rights?' ask Nicaraguan women in the run up to Beijing. Along with the rest of Central American women caught between a negligent state and the strictures of the Catholic hierarchy, they have little redress for the abuse, intimidation and violence that is common currency in their everyday lives.

In Nicaragua, where their status has regressed since the fall of the Sandinista government, women's organisations are attempting to fill the void created by church and state by educating women in their rights.

One of these, Red de Mujeres contra la Violencia, is a network of women's groups dealing with violence and abuse, particularly prevalent in the home. Another, Red de Mujeres por la Salud, concentrates on health

Isola
He controls your activ who you see, who you to. He won't let you your friends or family, o them visit you. He h your things, eavesdrop your conversations, he w let you go out on your o

Sexual abuse
He makes you perform sexual acts against your will. He treats you like a sex object. He never takes your desires or your needs into account. He hurts you physically and emotionally during the sex act.

Physical violence
pulling your hair, pushing, slapping, hitting, biting, twisting your arm, kicking. stabbing, slashing, shooting, burning, killing

Thre
He threatens you if you you're thinking of leav him. He says he's goin hurt you, or kill you that he'll kill himself. says you'll lose your ho or your child

THE BODY POLITIC: NICARAGUA

problems, sex education and birth control. A typical meeting at the Centros Alternativos de Mujeres in Managua this year, included workshops on death in childbirth, teenage pregnancy, dangers in pregnancy and childbirth and the health risks associated with back street abortions, from which thousands die each year, and to which most women are condemned given the Catholic ban on contraception, reiterated by the Pope early in July. Workshops also covered contraceptive methods and general dietary and health advice.

The chart alongside is from *What to do and where to go in case of violence*, produced by Red de Mujeres contra la Violencia, whose publications in simple language and graphically presented are beginning to reach a wide audience. The network also provides refuges for the victims of domestic violence. ❑

...tional abuse
...makes you feel that you ...do anything right, or ...you're crazy. He ...es you for everything. ...makes fun of you, ...ules you or humiliates ...n front of your family, ...ds, or strangers.

Economic abuse
He doesn't let you work outside the home. If you want to buy anything, you have to ask him for money. He accuses you of stealing his money when he doesn't give you enough to get by on.

Domestic slavery
He treats you like a servant, gives you no help with the housework, or with the children. He makes you treat him like a king in his kingdom.

...timidation
...e scares you by the way ...looks at you, by the way ...acts, by screaming, ...rowing things, destroying ...ur things. He won't let ...u out of the house, or ...to the house.

TIBET
A state-owned womb

China initiated its birth-control policy in Tibet in 1982 by imposing abortions or exorbitant fines on women becoming pregnant 'without permission' or having more children than regional quotas allowed... Confusing and ambiguous guidelines were issued that imply, but never state, that a birth without permission is a punishable offence.

In October 1994, the severe Mother and Child Health Law was adopted by the National People's Congress to take effect in 1995. Under this law, Chinese officials reserve the right to prevent marriages and births based on what they determine as the mental and physical state of the parents... People suffering from mental and contagious diseases will have to defer their marriages when the diseases are serious and likely to affect others. Those who still elect to marry must comply with lifelong contraceptive measures or undergo ligation. This would include children of political prisoners interred in psychiatric hospitals... It also stipulates that foetuses carrying hereditary diseases or seriously abnormal should be terminated, and women who have already given birth to defective infants will be subjected to medical examinations to determine whether they will be granted permission to conceive again... Decisions about the women's reproductive future is made by a governing body of medical staff and not in consultation with the woman or her family.

Methods of physical coercion
There is evidence that coercion is sometimes used by the Chinese to enforce birth-control policies. Local officials and doctors have quotas they must fulfil. They are rewarded monetarily if these are met; punished if they are not. Even women who are permitted to have another child are sometimes tricked or forced into 'birth-control operations' to enable these quotas to be met.
- **Abortion** — forced or voluntary; compulsory for couples with hereditary diseases; compulsory for unregistered couples or those without birth permits issued by the Chinese authorities
- **Sterilisation** — conducted without consent and often performed when women enter hospital for other surgery or medical treatment
- **Infanticide** — immediately following birth.

THE BODY POLITIC: TIBET

Chinese authorities make no attempt to educate Tibetan women on alternative and less drastic methods of contraception. No evidence exists that the Chinese have attempted any form of population control other than surgical procedures. While abortions are the widest form of contraception employed in Tibet, they are often conducted without proper equipment or anaesthetic in unhygienic conditions and the medical complications that follow are immense, sometimes resulting in death.

Economic penalties

Women are often given the 'option' of either paying an enormous fine or terminating the pregnancy. The economic well-being of Tibetan families is seriously endangered by the economic penalties imposed by the Chinese for breaching the law. The following penalties effectively violate a Tibetan woman's right to reproductive choice:

- heavy fines — usually the equivalent of over five years' income
- loss of job
- demotion or disqualification from potential promotion
- cuts in salary.

Tashi Dolma: Tibetan doctor whose child was forcibly aborted

A Tibetan child born outside Chinese regulations will be denied legal papers as well as the right to attend school, own property, travel, participate in organised work or obtain a ration card. The latter is essential for the monthly allotment of Tibetan dietary staples at government stores.

Chinese birth-control policies serve not only as a means of controlling Tibetan women's bodies but represent a pillar of China's colonial policy to reduce Tibetans to a minority in their own country.

International and human rights organisations remain the only actors able to rally against China's onslaught against Tibetans as a distinct cultural group. ❑

From A State-Owned Womb: Violations of Tibetan Women's Reproductive Rights *(Tibetan Women's Association, Dharamsala, India, 1995)*

UNESCO

ALGERIA
Why women?

A year ago, (*Index* 4&5 1994) Aïcha Lemsine wrote: 'In Bosnia rape became a tactical weapon of war in pursuit of ethnic cleansing; here the final solution against women has become a terrorist strategy for cleansing religion.'

In that year, women became the ultimate prize disputed among Algeria's warring factions. Girls were killed by Islamic extremists because they did not wear the veil; by the anti-Islamic, 'Organisation of Young Algerians' because they did: 'for every woman killed for not wearing the veil we shoot three who wear it'; because they were 'the wives, mothers and daughters of policemen or soldiers' and because, according to the Armed Islamic Group, 'Women should not stay with their husbands if these men have renounced the faith by supporting tyranny.'

Any excuse is used to terrorise women: those with jobs regarded as 'ungodly', such as fortune-tellers, were killed; hairdressers were murdered to force others to close down their salons, described by the Islamists as 'dens of iniquity'; women magistrates, court clerks and lawyers were sentenced to death for 'collaboration'; female journalists and media employees were mowed down along with their male counterparts.

Why the women? *Violence*, published by Unesco in June to mark the second anniversary of the murder of Tahar Djaout, the first journalist killed in Algeria, suggests that 'It is through women that the opening up and development of society has taken shape. The fundamentalists cannot confirm their hold on the country without cutting women down to size.'

According to official figures released on 20 February this year, 365 women and 59 children have been murdered. These are only the known victims of terrorism. Domestic violence and murder in the homes of women who refuse to bow to the Islamic dictates of male family members are uncounted. The number of rape cases and kidnappings is impossible to establish. Teenage girls have been taken hostage, held for weeks, even months, and subjected to gang-rape. And the violence continues. The following women are some of its latest victims:

November 1994: **Zoulikha** and **Saida Boughadou**, secondary school pupils, had their throats slashed in public along with their mother near Sidi M'hamed, near Algiers. The father, sons and another daughter were spared. The 'emir' —

Islamist strongman — was the village blacksmith and one of the kidnappers was a neighbour's son. One villager close to the terrorists explained: 'Boughadou refused to follow our recommendations about the education of his daughters. He went on sending them to school although we had forbidden it. He wouldn't listen.'

December: A young woman civil servant was kidnapped in El-Harrach, a working-class suburb of Algiers. Her husband was shown her decapitated and mutilated body at the morgue a few days later. Her torturers had sewn a man's head into her insides.

15 February 1995: **Nabila Djahnine**, an architect and president of a women's association in Kabylia, was shot with a hunting rifle in Tizi-Ouzou.

12 March: sisters **Karina** (21) and **Anna** (18) **Guedjali** were shot and killed in Reghaia, 20 miles east of Algiers, in front of their mother. One of the sisters had been engaged to a policeman.

12 March: At nightfall eight armed men broke into a house in Tessala El-Merdja, near Blida, while the owner was out. They shot his wife, 26-year-old **Yasmina Amrani**, who was eight months pregnant, at point-blank range.

14 March: **Fatima Ghodbane** (15), daughter of a retired civil servant, was dragged from her classroom by six armed men. They cut her throat about 10 metres outside Mohamed Lazhar secondary school.

15 March: **Saliha Laaroumi**, a woman magistrate and head of the court in Larbaa, 20 miles south of Algiers, was murdered.

16 March: Three girls had their throats slashed in an Algiers park opposite Ryad-el-Feth, the capital's main shopping centre.

Despite the terror, women continue to be a source of hope. The only major demonstrations calling for peace and an end to the killings have been initiated by women. Many women, particularly among the artistic community — film makers, theatre directors, actresses, singers, writers — have been forced into exile; their work is banned and reviled, their lives and those of their families is repeatedly threatened, gruesome hate-mail arrives in the post. Others, unable or unwilling to leave, refuse to give up the fight. 'Given the choice betweeen living as a second-class citizen somewhere else and dying here, I still choose to die in my own country,' is a view shared by many of Algeria's women. 'Women are the only men in this country,' comments a high-ranking male official. 'They are still struggling to live, whereas most men have to all intents and purposes given up the fight.' ❏

Compiled by Judith Vidal-Hall from Violence *(Unesco, July 1995), available in French or English*

ANNA J ALLOTT

BURMA
'If you can wait'

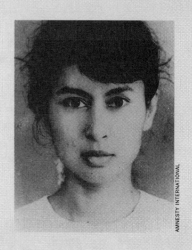

On 10 July, Burmese opposition leader and 1991 Nobel peace prize winner, Aung San Suu Kyi, was freed after almost six years under house arrest. Reports say she was informed by Deputy Intelligence Chief Colonel Kyaw Win that she was, henceforth, 'free to go anywhere, meet anyone', just like an ordinary Burmese citizen — provided she did not violate the law.

The sudden release, long demanded by governments around the world, took diplomats and the international media by surprise. The State Law and Order Restoration Council's apparent change of heart may be the result of pressure from the Japanese and US governments and from Nelson Mandela and the Socialist International now meeting in South Africa. The threat of further UN sanctions, the desperate need for the foreign investment that is not forthcoming because of the government's appalling human rights record and fears for the success of its 'Visit Myanmar (Burma) 1996' tourist drive, may equally have played their part in SLORC's decision to attempt a refurbishment of its image.

However, given the government-controlled media, repressive censorship laws that forbid all criticism of the military and the ban on unauthorised public meetings of more than five people (*Index* 3/1994), only time will tell how long Aung San Suu Kyi will be able to avoid 'violating the law'. She is loved and admired throughout Burma; as with Nelson Mandela, thousands will want to see her. They will also have high expectations from her new 'freedom'.

At the press conference she held on her release, citing the 'once bitter enemies in South Africa [who] are now working together for the betterment of their people', she appealed for reconciliation and for political change through dialogue. She warned that Burma faced a choice between this or 'utter devastation'. She also urged the authorities to 'release those of us who still remain in prison.' ❑

Anna J Allott is senior research fellow in Burmese studies at the School of Oriental and African Studies, London University

Julian Barnes
Lionel Blue
Joseph Brodsky
A S Byatt
Beatrix Campbell
Noam Chomsky
Alan Clark
Emma Donoghue
Ariel Dorfman
Ronald Dworkin
Umberto Eco
James Fenton
Paul Foot
Zufar Gareev
Timothy Garton Ash
Nadine Gordimer
Gunter Grass
Vaclav Havel
Christopher Hitchens
Ryszard Kapuscinski
Yasar Kemal
Helena Kennedy
Ivan Klima
Doris Lessing
Mario Vargas Llosa
Naguib Mahfouz
Alberto Manguel
Arthur Miller
Caroline Moorehead
Aryeh Neier
Harold Pinter
Jane Regan
Salman Rushdie
Edward Said
Posy Simmonds
John Simpson
Alexander Solzhenitsyn
Wole Soyinka
Stephen Spender
Tatyana Tolstaya
Alex de Waal
Edmund White
Vladimir Zhirinovsky

'**INDEX** *has bylines that Vanity Fair would kill for. Would that bylines were the only things about* **INDEX** *people were willing to kill for.*'

—Boston Globe

United Kingdom & Overseas (excluding USA & Canada)

		UK:		Overseas:		Students: £25
1 year—6 issues			£32		£38	
2 years—12 issues			£59		£70	
3 years—18 issues			£85		£105	

Name

Address

Postcode

£ _____ total.

❏ Cheque (£)   ❏ Visa/Mastercard   ❏ Am Ex   ❏ Diners Club

Card No.

Expiry   Signature   B5A4

❏ I would also like to send **INDEX** to a reader in the developing world—just £22. These sponsored subscriptions promote free speech around the world for only the cost of printing and postage.

Return to: INDEX, Freepost, 33 Islington High Street, London N1 9BR
Telephone: 0171 278 2313   **Facsimile:** 0171 278 1878

United States and Canada

	US$:	Students: $35
1 year—6 issues	$48	
2 years—12 issues	$90	
3 years—18 issues	$136	

Name

Address

Postcode

$ _____ total.

❏ Cheque (US$)   ❏ Visa/Mastercard   ❏ Am Ex   ❏ Diners Club

Card No.

Expiry   Signature   B5B4

❏ I would also like to send **INDEX** to a reader in the developing world—just $33. These sponsored subscriptions promote free speech around the world for only the cost of printing and postage.

INDEX ON CENSORSHIP

33 Islington High Street, London N1 9LH England   Facsimile: 0171 278 2313

BUSINESS REPLY SERVICE
Licence No. LON 6323

INDEX ON CENSORSHIP
33 Islington High Street
London N1 9BR
United Kingdom

NO POSTAGE
NECESSARY
IF MAILED
IN THE
UNITED STATES

BUSINESS REPLY MAIL
FIRST CLASS PERMIT NO.7796 NEW YORK, NY

Postage will be paid by addressee.

INDEX ON CENSORSHIP
c/o Fund for Free Expression
485 Fifth Avenue
NEW YORK, NY   10164-0709

THE BODY POLITIC: PHOTO FEATURE

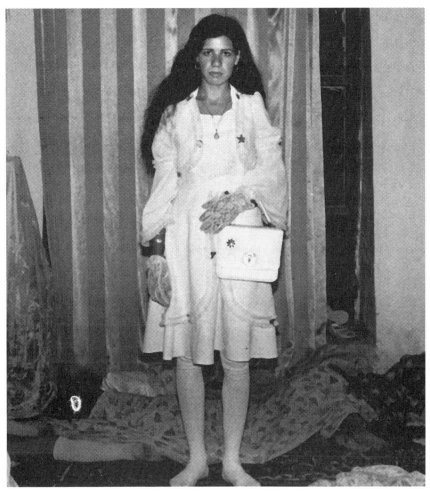

1) In Mishian, a small village in the district of Khomein, Iran, Akram, the 16-year-old bride poses in her wedding dress. Everything, down to the handbag, has been hired for the day

Wedding in Khomein

Credit: All photographs by Hengameh Golestan

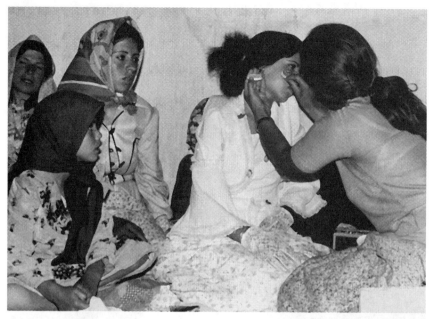

2) ...and puts on a good face

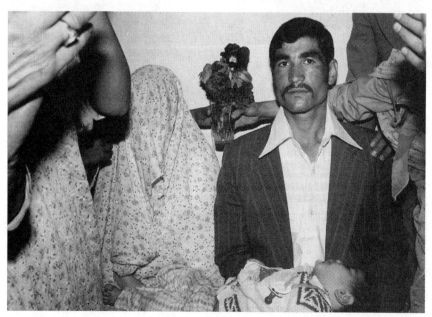

3) Eighteen-year-old husband Ahmad is presented to the women. The following week he returned to the Iran-Iraq front. The baby — an auspicious symbol of the bride's hoped for fertility — has been loaned for the occasion

4) Last minute words of advice and warning from the experienced brides of last year
5) Kokab, entertainer at the feast: singer, dancer, musician and family friend

...and in the suburbs of Teheran

6) Yesterday she was at school, today it's her wedding day. Seventeen-year-old Susan flanked by the aunts

7) Waiting for the mullah with Marhamat Khanum, matchmaker, wise woman and factotum of the suburb

8) Monir, sister of the bride celebrates with the women. Her mother — winner of a prize samovar for bearing the most children in the neighbourhood, 13 — with grandchild

9) Apprehension on the threshold

BABEL

Continuing our series focusing on the voices of those silenced by poverty, prejudice and exclusion

FELIX CORLEY

A small war you may have missed

By the time Moscow took on General Dudayev and the Chechens, it had already made war on another Caucasian people. Its success against the Ingush went unremarked

There was something all too familiar: women, their faces haunted by a look of hidden agony, were telling of how their menfolk had been taken from them, killed, beaten, taken hostage, how there had been no news of them for months or years. They show me photographs of their menfolk, wearing their best clothes or their army uniforms, in the classic poses beloved of Soviet photographers.

This is Russia's troubled southern border along the North Caucasus. The women are Ingush, driven from their homes in the Prigorodny district in the republic of North Ossetia by the North Ossetian forces with the connivance and active support of Russian troops. For years the Ingush — the majority in the district — had suffered harassment and discrimination at the hands of the Ossetians. In late 1992, they organised a peaceful campaign asking that the district — home to some 75,000 people, mostly Ingush — be returned to Ingush control.

The Prigorodny district descended rapidly into war. The North Ossetian authorities claimed the Ingush were preparing bandit raids against them with the help of their ethnic brothers, the Chechens. Irregular bands of Ossetian thugs, backed up by Russian troops, moved in. Hundreds died in bitter clashes, most of them Ingush. Within days, 60,000 Ingush were driven across the border into the neighbouring republic of Ingushetia with little more than the clothes they stood up in. Ingush homes were looted and burned; their charred remains litter the district today. Hundreds of Ingush were seized by Ossetian forces during and after the fighting. Many remain unaccounted for.

There are some 240,000 Ingush, the majority in Ingushetia. They are Sunni Muslims, ethnically close to the Chechens. In 1992, following the disintegration of the USSR, Ingushetia, having elected to remain within the Russian Federation, separated from the newly independent republic of Chechnya.

Almost three years later, many of the refugees — or deportees, as they correctly insist they should be called — have moved in with relatives in Ingushetia. Many more, who have no family they can shelter with, have been crammed into makeshift refugee camps on the edge of Nazran, capital of Ingushetia. In summer, frequent rains turn the settlements into seas of mud. In winter, the huts are freezing. Water is fetched from a standpipe at the edge of the camp. Life is miserable, with little in the way of state handouts and limited help from foreign charities.

Ingush President Ruslan Aushev has warned of rising tension over the Russian government's failure to recover the Prigorodny district or secure the deportees' return. Without massive pressure from Moscow the Ossetians will never agree to reverse the success of their particular version of ethnic cleansing. If they can keep the Ingush out they will be able to retain ownership of the area they took over from Ingush-Chechen control when both peoples were deported — along with other Caucasian nations — beyond the Urals by Stalin in 1944. The Ingush began to return from Central Asia in 1957; Prigorodny district, by now resettled with Ossetians, was never returned to Chechen-Ingush jurisdiction.

But Moscow has more serious problems on its mind: alongside the mayhem in Chechnya, the problems of the Ingush are a minor, easily forgotten tragedy to which no-one is offering a solution. The Chechen-Russian war has swollen the refugee population in Ingushetia by at least 100,000, the bulk of them Chechens, who are now living in camps. Ingush fleeing the destruction of Grozny have joined the earlier exodus from Prigorodny.

Mariam Arapieva, *refugee and camp organiser, husband killed*

'We weren't prepared for the fighting in 1992. The Ossetians did it, but Russia directed it all. They were behind it. My husband was killed, my house was ransacked and destroyed. Here in the camp I have 15 or 16 families who've lost up to five or six people. Sons who have disappeared. Children attacked, their tongues cut out, ears cut off — we left some in hospital in Grozny... Thousands of our children were killed, but we haven't killed even one child of theirs.

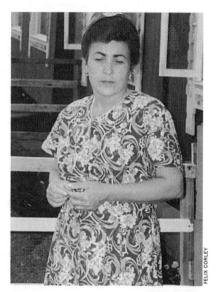

Mariam Arapieva

'Up until 1991 relations between the Ossetians and the Ingush were good, we lived in friendship. There were some conflicts, of course, as there always are anywhere. But in 1991 many people were suddenly sacked from their jobs, a ban on buying houses, a ban on being registered to live in the district — just against the Ingush. Then they stripped naked a young girl, and that's how it started. They did anything to get it going. We trusted them up till then. But as to living in peace with the Ossetians again, I can't say it's possible.

'There are 851 people registered here in the camp. In summer it's very hot and impossible to breathe. In winter the wooden huts are freezing. There are many sick people, many invalids. And during the school holidays there is nothing for the children, no pioneer camps, no holiday camps, there's no way of clothing them, getting shoes for them. The problem is our republic of Ingushetia is young, it has nowhere to get money to provide for our people. There are many camps like this here in Nazran.

'Local people here help us, people who once lived in the Prigorodny district, and there are good lads who're working in Moscow — they help us a lot. Thanks to them we're surviving. Without them I don't know what we'd do.

'Russia's president has issued decrees ordering the return of the refugees to the district. The people don't understand why not one decree has been carried out.

'The main thing is that we want to return home to the Prigorodny district. Although many people have been killed and our homes have been destroyed, whatever is there, even if there is only one stone still standing, we want to go back to the land of our ancestors, our parents. This isn't just my feeling, it's the feeling of everyone here, from the children up. Even if we have to die we will return to our homes.

'We trust only in the Great Allah, there's no-one else we put our trust in. We've lost all our other hope.'

Pyatimat Buruzheva, *refugee, husband and three sons disappeared*

'From 1957 until 1992 I lived in the village of Oktyabrskoye. We lived in peace there. War started on 3 November. Ossetian bandits — about five or six of them — came to the house at about four in the afternoon. They took my husband Osman and our three sons. They took 17 people, just from our street. From the village of Oktyabrskoye 64 people have disappeared without trace. Since then we've had no news of them or where they are. I don't know if they're dead or alive, but if you want to know I could tell you who took them from the house.

'I've written so many letters, so many complaints. I've knocked on so many doors. But up till now there has been no reply. I've gone to Moscow twice and handed in appeals to so many offices.

'Each time the Russian investigators come here, they say they don't have the right to go to investigate there. It seems the Ossetians are more powerful than the Russians, than Yeltsin.

'We will definitely go back there, to live on our land. We're not asking for Ossetian land. May God ensure that my sons and my husband will return and we can all go back.'

Movlatkhan Buruzheva, *refugee, husband, son and sister-in-law disappeared*

'I'm from the same village of Oktyabrskoye and my family too has disappeared. When it all started they took my husband Magomed, my son and my sister-in-law, who's psychologically disturbed. We don't know where they took them. We know who took them. We've spoken about it, written letters to everyone, to Yeltsin, but there's been no reply. Not one.

'They stole everything we'd built up over many years, burnt our houses. I've got nothing left to lose. We live here in wooden huts. There's no work. Nothing.

'The Ossetians destroyed our family, they've destroyed people who didn't know what weapons were, who worked hard all their lives and lived honestly. But they just did what they liked to them. Killed men, old people and children, and threw their bodies to the pigs [as Muslims, Ingush refuse to keep or eat pigs]. They've no human feelings, they're worse than animals.'

Leila Doskhoieva, *refugee, seven children, husband disappeared*

'On 3 November 1992 I was going by train from Vladikavkaz to Moscow. They dragged me from the train and took me hostage. I was held for almost a week in Kartsa. There were about 600 hostages there. A young man died in front of my eyes and they just threw his body out. Young girls there who were raped. People were killed.

'When they exchanged us we had to walk across the mountains. I arrived here on 9 November and found out my husband wasn't here. I don't know where he is. I have seven children and no work. The oldest is 23, he doesn't work. Eight of us live together in one hut.

Leila Amerkhanova, *refugee, aged 33, three young children, husband disappeared*

'We lived in a flat in the centre of Vladikavkaz. We didn't know anything about the troubles. They took us all — my husband, me and the children — as hostages. My husband was very tall, 1.92 metres, and was a sportsman.

'We were all kept in a cellar, about a thousand of us. There was very little food and not enough water, only enough for the children. The adults went without. At the windows of the cellars they placed machine guns. If you stuck your head out they opened fire with tracer bullets. They came down at night, picked out the healthy men and the pretty girls.

BABEL: INGUSHETIA

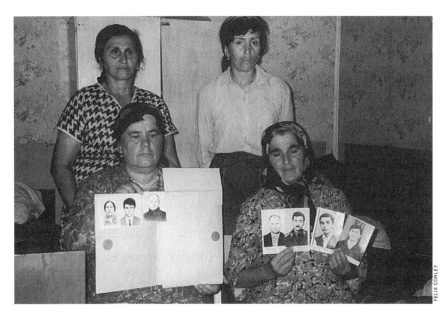

Women without men: 75 per cent of the world's refugees are women and children

'When they picked out my husband, they beat him. Twice it happened. When they came about midnight — there were about 25 of them — we hid him. They called out people's names according to a list, but if they didn't find someone they just grabbed someone else. Since they took him I haven't had any news. Some people say he's been shot, others say he hasn't. They beat my nine-year-old boy on the legs as if he was an adult. We've had to take him to the doctor three times.

'And they are still holding hostages, 189 of them, and there's been no news of them. All this is nothing other than ethnic cleansing, genocide. Look at our young people, they're all psychologically damaged. Here there's just women and children. We've nowhere else to go.

'They keep shouting about how there are human rights in Russia. But have a look, blood is being spilt. Wherever Russia interferes, there's blood, Afghanistan, Korea, Vietnam... They want to destroy the small nations. Yeltsin issues decrees but they're not fulfilled. They don't want to fulfil them. Why hasn't our case been raised in international forums?' ❑

Felix Corley *is a writer on eastern Europe and a regular visitor to the Caucasus*

MINORITIES

VIRGINIA LULING

People of the clay

'We were born poor, making and selling pots. My parents had land. The Hutus took it. No-one listens to us. The government ignores our complaints, so do the courts. We Batwa, we are humiliated.' (Twa, Rwanda, 1993)

'When I wanted to build my residence, I had the bush burnt. The place was inhabited by Twa. Their huts caught fire, a few people died. The rest moved further off.' (Tutsi chief, Burundi, 1950s)

Reports of the 1994 bloodbath in Rwanda, and the violence in neighbouring Burundi, have made an international audience aware of the Tutsi and Hutu and their murderous rivalry. Little attention, however, has been paid to the third 'tribe' or caste in those countries, the Twa, or Batwa. (Ba-twa designates the Twa people; an individual is a Mutwa.)

The Twa are among the 'Pygmy' peoples of central Africa, the indigenous people of the Great Lakes region. Though small in stature, most are not so small as to be easily distinguished from the rest of the population. Though it is not clear how long they have been there, they were certainly hunting and foraging in the forests before the farming villagers arrived in the early centuries of this era, and, rather later, the cattle-keeping aristocracy. These two groups are known by various names throughout the region, but in Rwanda and Burundi they are the Hutu and Tutsi.

Before 1994 there were 30,000 or more Twa in Rwanda, an estimated 56,000 in Burundi and a smaller but uncertain number in Uganda and eastern Zaire. They represent the last stage of a process now threatening their relatives, the 'Pygmy' peoples of the forests of central Africa. Logging and agriculture are eating away the forest that is their home, but

MINORITIES: TWA

Twa potters, Rwanda 1993: 'wherever there is clay there are Batwa'

in no African state are they accorded any legal rights in it. Once the forest is destroyed, they are left without land or resources.

Until recently, some Twa were able to continue as hunters and gatherers in the remains of the highland forests around the Great Lakes; very few still do. Much of the forest was cut down long ago to make way for farming and cattle-herding, and most of the remainder has gone in the last 30 years. Deprived of their livelihood as hunters and generally landless, the Twa became potters. This is now so much part of their character that they have been called 'the people of the clay'. 'Wherever there is clay there are Batwa.' But the introduction of plastic and metal containers has ruined their market.

> Clay used to give me meat which I could eat with other things,
> Clay gave me sorghum and I could drink sorghum beer.
> Clay gave me beans I could eat very well with lots of other things...
>   Ayee!...
> The plastic cups and dishes and pans have come...
> Clay, clay, you have no more value...
> Here are the plastic cups and dishes, the aluminium saucepans.
> You have given no value to clay.
>   Aaayeeeeee.....! *(Rwandan Twa song)*

The Twa are the lowest caste in society, looked down on by both Tutsi and Hutu. The discrimination takes many forms: access to public wells is forbidden them; a cup or dish which a Twa has used is 'untouchable' and may be broken to avoid re-use. There are many reports of Batwa being wounded or even killed because they had managed to acquire some land or a few goods.

As well as potters, the Twa, who have the musical gift of all the 'Pygmy' peoples, are famous as musicians and dancers. Like other oppressed peoples, they are admired as entertainers, without this raising their status otherwise. Most Twa remain the poorest of the poor, almost entirely without schooling, and without any voice in the politics of their countries.

There were exceptions: in the days of the old Kingdoms of Rwanda and Burundi, and the other kingdoms in what are now Uganda and Tanzania, some Twa became favoured servants of the Kings, acting as soldiers as well as singers and entertainers. The relationship could be a close one; most of the royal houses are known to have Twa blood in their veins. But with the fall of the monarchies in the run-up to independence in the 1950s and '60s, these favoured ones — who had only ever been a minority — lost everything. In Rwanda in particular, all that remains is the resentment that such favouritism had engendered, and the suspicion among the Hutu that the Twa were 'friends — lackeys — of the Tutsi'.

German colonisation of Rwanda and Burundi in the 1880s, inherited by Belgium after World War I, sharpened the inequality between Tutsi and Hutu and gave it a racist underpinning. With the departure of the colonial power in 1962, it mutated into the bloody rivalry that has claimed millions of victims since the 1960s. In this violence, the Twa have been both pawns and victims.

The same poverty and discrimination shown the Twa of Rwanda affects the Twa in neighbouring countries. But Rwanda's Twa are so far the only group among the 'Pygmy' peoples to have set up their own organisation in an attempt to improve their economic and social situation. The *Association pour la Promotion des Batwa* (APB), set up in 1991, had a troubled start, but by 1993, it had formed links with western NGOs and indigenous organisations in other countries, and started various projects such as a workshop training for young people in tailoring and carpentry.

All that ended on 6 April 1994, when the plane carrying the presidents of Rwanda and Burundi crashed and 30 years of bloodshed reached their climax in the genocide by Hutu extremists of the Tutsi and all others who stood in their way. The Twa community has been reduced by an estimated one-third — 10,000 people. Whole villages have vanished. Often they were targeted as supposed supporters of the invading Rwandan Patriotic Front (RPF), or more generally as 'friends of the Tutsi'. Another 8,000-10,000 have fled the country and are in the refugee camps of Zaire and Tanzania where they fare even worse than other refugees.

Most Twa remain the poorest of the poor, without schooling and without any voice in the politics of their countries

The Twa also took part in the massacres; they had little choice. One man was told: 'We are going to kill all your family if you don't bring us three Tutsi heads.' This in turn laid the whole community open to revenge by the RPF forces as they took over the country. Today, it is above all the Twa *men* who are missing; dead or fled.

The present Rwandan government is, as far as policies go, more favourable to the Twa than any of its predecessors. But in Rwanda today, policies have little impact on reality. The absence of any proper justice as yet for the crimes of 1994 leaves the field clear for random denunciations and acts of revenge, and the Twa are easy victims.

The fate of the Twa both in and outside Rwanda depends on that of the region as a whole, where there is certainly more violence to come. At present their best hope may lie in the Rwandan indigenous organisation, now reconstituted under a new name. If this can survive to become an effective force, it may yet help all the 'people of the clay' to find their voice. ❑

Virginia Luling works for Survival International, a worldwide organisation supporting the right of tribal peoples to decide their own future and helping in the protection of their lives, lands and human rights. Survival is working for the rights of the Twa and the other 'Pygmy' peoples

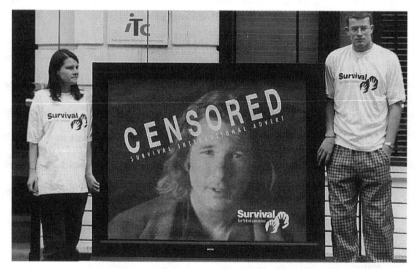

London 1995: Survival anti-ban protest

On the line: 1,2,3. *New Internationalist*; 4,5,6,7. *The Facts About Women, Women's Action Coalition* (New Press, New York); 8. *Population and Reproductive Rights; Feminist Perspectives from the South*, Sonia Correa in collaboration with Rebecca Reichmann, (Zed Books/DAWN); 9,10. *Girls and Women: A UNICEF Development Priority*, (Programme Publications, UN Children Fund); 11. *Harpers*; 12,13. *Women's Health: Across Age and Frontier*, (World Health Organisation); 14,15,16. Heise 'Violence against women: the missing agenda' in Koblinsky et al *The Health of Women; a Global Perspective*; 17. *Chemical Marketing Reporter*, 18. UN Secretariat on 4th Conference on Women; 19,20,21. UN Secretariat; 22. Women's World Summit Foundation; 23. *Iran Bulletin*; 24. *Women and Politics Worldwide*; 25. Charles Humana, *World Human Rights Guide*; 26. *Women and Develpment Worldwide*; 27,28. Amnesty International; 29. Reuters; 30. *Independent*; 31. Women's World Summit Foundation; 32. Charles Humana, *World Human Rights Guide*; 33. UN Fund For Population Activity; 34,35. Tatyana Mamonova *Women's Glasnost vs. Naglost*; 36. *Monitor*; 37. Reuters; 38. US Senate Committee on Judiciary; 39. *National Business Woman*; 40. *New York Times*; 41. *LA Times*; 42. *Guardian*; 43,44,45,46,47,48,49. Naomi Wolf, *The Beauty Myth;* 50. World Health Organisation

AIDAN RANKIN
Third time lucky?

The Independent Television Commission has asked UK TV companies to stop showing a Survival International advertisement on the grounds that Survival is a 'political' organisation and as such is prohibited from advertising on British screens.

Singling out the indigenous populations of Amazonia, the Buddhist Chakmas of Bangladesh and the Aborigines of Australia, the advertisement has the actor Richard Gere describing the threat to tribal peoples from the 'forces of so-called civilisation'. Gere asks his audience to donate to or become members of Survival, the only organisation dedicated to campaigning for tribal peoples worldwide.

Rule 10 of the ITC's Advertising Code, already invoked against *Index on Censorship* and Amnesty International, prohibits advertisements 'by or on behalf of any body whose objects are wholly or mainly of a political nature'. Political activity is defined as aiming to 'influence legislation or action by central or local government'.

Survival's activities are wholly within the guidelines issued by the Charity Commissioners. These draw a rigorous distinction between political and humanitarian activities. The ITC's evidence in support of their 'interim view' offered only a cursory and highly selective interpretation of a Survival brochure. It ignored Survival's role in public education and field projects, including the funding of medical aid. It also chose to overlook the fact that our campaigning activities are directed at multinational companies and multilateral development banks at least as much as national governments.

While the ITC ruling is not an official ban, British television companies are nonetheless forced to withdraw the advertisement until Survival produces 'evidence' that it does not contravene Rule 10. Meanwhile, despite the UK television ban, the Gere advertisement is being shown on television and in cinemas throughout Europe in one of the biggest cinema charity campaigns ever launched. ❑

Aidan Rankin is *Campaigns Press Officer at Survival International*

Cuba redux

Cuba's resurgent civil society groups are trying to spark a debate on the country's urgent economic and social problems. But breaking down the old Cold War polarities is a dangerous business. A report from Cuba compiled by Adam Newey

Left: Paul Schatzberger/Panos Pictures   *All uncredited translations by Adam Newey*

Official name: República de Cuba
Administrative division: 14 provincias, divided into 169 municipios
Capital: Ciudad de la Habana (Havana), population 2,100,000 (1989 estimate)
Population (1993): 10,900,000
Head of state: Fidel Castro Ruz, constitutional head of state since 2 December 1976, although de facto leader since 1959. Titles: President of the Council of State and Council of Ministers, Secretary-General of the Communist Party and Commander-in-Chief of the Revolutionary Armed Forces

Constitution: Cuba's socialist constitution states that 'all the power belongs to the working people and is exercised through the Assemblies of People's Power'
The *Asamblea Nacional de Poder Popular*, with 589 members (1993), is elected by the people every five years. the 30 member *Consejo de Estado* and the 44-member *Consejo de Ministros* are the two highest government bodies
Political parties: Cuban Communist Party (PCC), the 'supreme leading force of society and state', is the only legal political party
Urbanisation (1992): 75%
Age structure: one in three Cubans is under 26
Social development index: UNDP Human Development Index (1994): 89 (in 'medium human development' category); UK 10, USA 8
Ethnic composition: officially 66% Hispanic, 12% black, 21.9% mulatto (mixed Hispanic and black) and 0.1% Asian
Language: Spanish, with regional variations affecting both accent and vocabulary
Religion: there is no established church. Some Cubans are Roman Catholic, there are many Protestant churches, and Afro-Cuban religions are very popular
Media and communications: 343 radios, 203 television sets and 56.4 telephones per 1,000 inhabitants (UK/US: 1,146/2,123 radios, 435/815 television sets, 477/789 telephones). Cuba has 5 national radio stations and one international network (Radio Habana Cuba) in addition to about 50 local stations. There are 2 national television networks, Cubavisión and Tele-Rebelde, which broadcast only in the evenings except on Sundays ❑

From Emily Hatchwell and Simon Calder Cuba in Focus: A Guide to the People, Politics and Culture *(Latin America Bureau, 1 Amwell St, London EC1R 1UL, July 1995, £5.99/US$12)*

ADAM NEWEY

No more heroes

Che Guevara was lucky. The CIA bullet that killed him in the Bolivian jungle in 1967 saved his reputation: posterity won't judge him by his faltering attempt to export Cuba's Revolution to the rest of Latin America. Instead, the Argentinian doctor became an icon, caught forever in Alberto Korda's famous snapshot at a defining moment of far-sighted vision and noble purpose, the deliverer of the Cuban people. Cuba's revolutionary pantheon had other gods, too: Frank País, Juan Almeida, Camilo Cienfuegos, all but forgotten now outside Cuba, and barely remembered inside. But Che never dies.

One of the first people I met in Havana was a man called Jorge, who sells copies of the Party newspaper *Granma* to tourists outside the Museum of the Revolution, fittingly housed in the beautiful old presidential palace. We sat down on the cool steps beneath the marble portico and talked. Times were hard, Jorge told me, five years into the 'special period' of economic restructuring, food rationing and shortages of just about everything, so he tried to supplement his state pension by offloading the occasional copy of *Granma*, strictly for dollars of course: tourists aren't supposed to carry Cuban pesos.

After a while, I thought I should buy one of Jorge's papers, so I handed him a dollar. A young tourist policewoman walked by just at that moment, gave us a rather inquisitive look and passed on. Part of their job is to protect tourists from harassment by the locals. Jorge leaned closer and whispered, 'Have you got one of these, a "Che"?' and handed me a bright 3-peso piece embossed with the familiar image, a little extra souvenir to take back home. At the official rate of exchange, he had just given me back three times what I had paid for the newspaper. It didn't matter, the face on the back was the valuable thing.

Jorge was one of the true believers. He'd spent half a life under a succession of petty dictators and megalomaniac autocrats, and the recollection of the revolutionaries riding in triumph into Havana in early January 1959 was crystal clear. 'Right down along here [the Paseo] they drove. I saw them all: Che, Camilo, Fidel.' Unlike Che, of course, Fidel Castro did what heroes shouldn't. He survived — the missile crisis, the Bay of Pigs, the Mariel boatlift, wars in Angola and Ethiopia, the collapse of international Communism, and the implacable US opposition to all that his Revolution stood for.

It's hard for Cubans to ignore the looming presence of their nearest neighbour to the north. Politics in Cuba is finely woven through with a strong nationalist thread, from the slogans on street walls ('We live in a free country!', 'I am happy because I am free!') to the cult of the one other hero who still commands universal adherence: José Martí, revolutionary, romantic poet, journalist and father of Cuban independence. The cult of Martí is particularly acute right now, in this the centenary year of his death in battle, at the very outset of Cuba's armed struggle for independence from Spain. That hero's death acts as a lightning rod to galvanise Cuban national pride, one that works powerfully in the current context of US policy towards Cuba.

The unhappy relationship between Cuba and the United States goes way back before 1959. In 1898, three years into a bitter war against Spain and with independence all but won, President McKinley sent a naval detachment to see off the remnants of the colonial forces on the island.

After a brief and decisive campaign, a peace treaty was signed between the United States and Spain, without any Cuban representation whatsoever.

The US intervention had been preceded by a fierce policy debate between those who believed Spain was best placed to protect US interests on the island, and others who favoured an independent Cuba, governed by proxy from Washington with a view to eventual annexation into the Union. The attitude towards Cubans themselves is well documented in instructions sent to the US military commander late in 1897:

'The inhabitants are generally indolent and apathetic,...indifferent to religion, and the majority are therefore immoral, have strong passions and are very sensual... It is obvious that the immediate annexation of these disturbing elements into our own federation in such large numbers would be sheer madness, so before we do that we must clean up the country, even if this means using the methods Divine Providence used on the cities of Sodom and Gomorrah. We must destroy everything within our cannons' range of fire. We must impose a harsh blockade so that hunger and its constant companion, disease, undermine the peaceful population and decimate the Cuban army...'

In the event, the first US-backed administrations were relatively benign. It was only in the 1920s and 1930s, as corruption set in, followed by the violent repression of Fulgencio Batista's second government, that another Cuban independence movement started to grow, with José Martí as a spiritual figurehead.

The symbols of Cuban independence are everywhere in Havana, put up by the Party to remind the people of what the current struggle is all about: despite the rhetoric, it's not about defending Communist ideology against the imperialist foe so much as bolstering national pride against aggressors of any stripe. Behind the symbols, behind the rhetoric, behind even the Party, there is the army, the Revolutionary Armed Forces (FAR), headed by Fidel Castro's younger brother Raul. Over the past year or so, FAR has been discreetly enhancing its role in society, helping out with the harvests, running factories, and opening a new chain of tourist shops. Cuba's revolutionary society has always been highly militarised, but in FAR's deeper reach into the civil infrastructure, it is hard not to discern an implicit threat.

Early on in my stay in Havana, I was vividly reminded of the stories my father told me about growing up under Nazi occupation in the

British Channel Islands. It wasn't just the rationing and the shortages, or the concomitant explosion of the black economy that were similar, nor the feeling of intense isolation, of being forgotten by the rest of the world, nor the powerlessness in the face of brute circumstance. More than any other single thing, it was a feeling of sheer boredom, which afflicts the young more especially than anybody. And I spent the rest of my time in Cuba trying to figure out exactly who the occupiers were in this analogy: was it the feared *norteamericanos*? The ubiquitous, all-embracing Party? Or was it us, the tourists?

Tourism is having a profound impact on the island. As the government tries to attract tourists in every greater numbers to shore up the economy, Cubans are becoming second-class citizens in their own country, powerless to stop the influx of dollars, driving down the real value of their pesos, watching as tourists spend money on goods and luxuries that they cannot hope to afford.

Havana 1993: 'Yes' to Cuba

Hence the explosion in prostitution: for young Cuban women, the only real chance of getting a piece of the tourist lifestyle — going to nightclubs, dinner in a hard-currency restaurant, perhaps some clothes — is to latch on to an unaccompanied male foreigner. The girls who trail after tourists, night after night — some as young as 12 or 13 — are known, not as *prostitutas*, but *jiniteras*, or 'jockeys'. They rarely if ever ask for money. And they know all about the risk of AIDS, but usually have to rely on the tourist to provide a condom. If he doesn't have one, they just take their chances.

Despite his improbable survival, Fidel Castro hasn't done so badly from the myth-makers, who have portrayed him as a man who needs barely four hours sleep a night, who can speak for eight or 10 hours at a stretch without notes, whose interest in the minutiae of government remains undimmed even after 36 years. Castro has frequently stressed his distaste for any cult of personality, but that hasn't stopped others creating one. The longer he goes on, however, the more the myth begins to crack, and awkward reality comes seeping through. I asked several people about their leader's fabled oratory stamina: could he really electrify an audience for so long? 'Well, no,' one student told me, 'most people find it a bit of a joke. The only reason so many go down to the Plaza de la Revolución and listen is that they always have a good party at the end. And we don't have too many parties nowadays.'

There's a prevailing sense of hopelessness among the young in Havana, which is a far cry from Che's enduring image of youthful fervour. It is those who were born since the Revolution, and who have gained most by it, who are least at ease with the sacrifices and privations that it now exacts. They are the ones who, a year ago, were willing to risk their lives on the flimsiest homemade craft to cross 90 miles of ocean in search of something better, or perhaps just something different.

The rafter crisis made great propaganda for the fierce anti-Castro lobby in Washington, those last of the cold warriors who regard the Florida Straits as another Berlin Wall: a defining line between freedom and tyranny. Over the years, both sides have been guilty of perpetuating the old bipolar divisions by resorting to the standard rhetoric: in Cuba, the state-controlled media unswervingly blame the crisis on the capitalist 'blockade'; while the US government broadcasts its own news and entertainment to the island from the Miami-based stations Radio Martí and TV Martí, purportedly to give Cubans access to something their own government denies them: hard news. Meanwhile, however, the

United States maintains a 25-year-old 'information embargo', which denies its own news bureaux the right to operate a base in Cuba.

Information, like everything else, is a scarce resource on the island. All broadcast media, all printing and publishing houses are owned and controlled by the state. A chronic paper shortage has meant that few books are now being published, and bookshops — aside from the dollar shops — are very poorly stocked. When I was there, in March, the American Association of Publishers had just opened an exhibition of Western books, the first of its kind in the country. There were some 5,000 different titles, arranged around the vast hall of the Capitol building in old Havana. There were medical books, engineering books, computing manuals, novels, social and political science books, children's books, even a copy of Fred Rogers's *You Are Special*: just about everything you could think of, and all of them were being donated to Cuban libraries at the end of the exhibition. This was clearly a laudable attempt to plug the information gap.

But I couldn't help thinking, as I wandered around the exhibition, looking at some of the familiar names on the covers, that Cuba's problems are Cuba's problems and outsiders can only do so much to help. I thought of Jorge and his awe at what his people had achieved for themselves, despite everything, and I realised that what Cuba desperately needs is a chance to sit down and have a serious talk with itself. That's very hard to do when every sphere of activity is controlled by the state, when at least 600 people, according to Amnesty International's very conservative estimation, are locked up for their political beliefs. But within the last year or so there has been a marked resurgence of activity among independent institutions — church groups, human rights groups, labour unions, journalists' associations — that have been emboldened by what appears to be a thaw in the government's attitude towards them. The recent release of Cuba's two most prominent dissidents, Yndamiro Restano and Sebastián Arcos, will further encourage them.

These groups are working hard, from widely variant ideological perspectives and practical experience, to establish a climate for dialogue, about where the country goes from here. Perhaps the old slogan 'Inside the Revolution, everything; outside the Revolution, nothing' is starting to lose its currency. Common throughout this nascent civil society is a recognition that heroes and slogans aren't enough any more, now that the world that gave birth to them has disappeared for good. ❏

MARTHA GELLHORN

Forty years on

'Back then the streets were full of half-starved people.., 40 years on, here they were, going to school, spotless, healthy, happy'

I went to live in Cuba in early '39, but was often away on war reporting. It was a beautiful climate, a very pleasant life. Intellectually moribund, but good for isolation and concentrating on writing.

I left for good in 1944 and did not revisit the island until 1986.

One of the first things that Castro did after the Revolution was to make an edict: he said 'there will be no more racism in this country', just like that, bingo. I spoke to a black woman writer to find out what really happens when someone says that there will be no more racism, that it's illegal. She said, well, it stopped. Perhaps the more we live together and see that we are not completely different kinds of beings, then it will be true in our hearts. But in effect it's true, because he just said it.

I think the real difference was that, having made this edict, blacks got equal wages, so that economically there was no apartheid, no discrimination in housing and so on. In the old days the racism was such that I literally didn't realise that Cuba was full of blacks, because the only black people who were allowed in Havana were housemaids. At the time of the Mardi Gras, suddenly there'd be an enormous number of black people prancing down the streets. I was astonished; where did they come from?

Well, that was a huge change. And, of course, back then the streets were full of half-starved people selling lottery tickets, and the street boys spent their time collecting cigarette butts and begging and selling newspapers. Then, 40 years later, here they all were in their school uniforms, going to school, looking spotless and healthy and happy. And no lottery tickets. Gambling is outlawed.

The Prado [the main boulevard in Old Havana] was full of old gents reading the newspaper and old ladies knitting on the benches, the kind of people you'd never have seen in Havana in a place like that. They existed, but one didn't know it.

Another edict was that anything that is essential for the people must be inexpensive, and books are essential so they cost less than an ice cream cone. Everyone could read now and the bookstores were always jammed, with all kinds of people, buying these cheap paperbacks. And there were many publishing houses, all belonging to the state, and all publishing different kinds of books, with a truly enormous output.

I went into several bookstores. In one of them, on a high shelf, in ugly red binding, was some Marx and Lenin. Clearly nobody ever bought them. I asked what the most popular books were, and they were detective stories and romances. In my day people couldn't read, and there was one bookshop in Havana, for the likes of us, mainly in English and possibly some in French and Spanish. The Cuban upper class didn't bother with reading, they were more interested in sports, or playing cards, or telling each other who married the second cousin of the third cousin's wife.

The great wave of tourism was after I left, after the war, and I missed the Batista dictatorship [1952-59]. When I was there, the government was just crooks. You'd come into town one day and hear shooting in the street, and the barman at the Floridita would say, 'Don't go out because they're having a coup.' So you sat and drank daiquiris until the shooting stopped and then there was another president. This didn't really inconvenience anybody, for the simple reason that it didn't matter who was in power, they were all the same. They were just booting each other out to get their hands in the trough.

Castro made a fool of the US over the Bay of Pigs. And he expropriated the property of Americans who made fortunes from their investments, but he didn't pay them any compensation. That was the terrible sin, because that was an attack on money. But then of course the Bay of Pigs was unforgivable, like Vietnam. American presidents seem to take defeat as a personal insult.

CUBA: FORTY YEARS ON

Isn't it maddening [the US policy]? What is there to do about it? There are so few people in America interested.

The idea that we have to starve the people of Cuba because they're led by a dangerous Communist is just ludicrous. I was thrilled by Cuba because all of a sudden women were equal in pay and responsibility, suddenly they had joined the twentieth century, rather ahead of other places. The sexes were, for once, in a normal relationship. People were self-confident and freer and happier than I remembered them.

Whereas we had a very nice life, it was almost a feudal society and although I was detached, living the life of the writer, at the same time there was something that made one basically uneasy. So in 1986 I thought Cuba was wonderful. It was the most socially advanced country in central and south America. ❏

Primary school Havana 1992: 'spotless, healthy, happy'

Martha Gellhorn *was born in St Louis, Missouri. In 1936 she published* The Trouble I've Seen, *her four linked novellas on Depression-hit America. Her reports from World War II Europe are included in* The Face of War

MARTA BEATRIZ ROQUE CABELLO
Let's talk about the Cuban economy

With the economy squeezed between the loss of Soviet cash and ever-tighter US sanctions, the government has to find another way

Thirty years ago, the 'green crocodile' of the Caribbean conjured up images of sugar and tobacco plantations, rum, bright sunshine and beautiful beaches. Today, Cuba is going through the worst economic crisis since independence. Far from affecting only the economy, it has had far-reaching social consequences.

At the start of the 1960s, Cuba began to direct the greater part of its commercial and financial efforts towards the Soviet Union and the other socialist countries of Europe. Now in the 1990s, all such efforts are directed towards beating off the threat of losing our current level of development. We have been plunged into a totally unfamiliar world: it speaks the language of the market-place and doesn't offer the facilities or preferential prices the former Soviet bloc offered. The loss of Soviet support alone has wiped out 75 per cent of the country's export capacity and overseas earnings.

So we need to find a way into the international community. From a purely commercial point of view, that entails solving a few problems first. Take the European Union, for example, and the kind of market that that could offer: its sheer distance puts our products at an immediate competitive disadvantage with respect to those of other countries closer to Europe. Then there are other hurdles, such as technical standards, environmental concerns, wrapping and packaging of goods, well-established quality parameters that we are not used to having to meet and that require extra investment. Further, since Cuba suspended debt repayments to Europe in the mid-1980s, several sources of credit have

I've already told you, I'll have no more subversive dreaming in this house! Okay?!

been closed to us, in particular those banks connected to the Paris Club of creditor nations. At present, Cuba's external debt with Europe runs at an estimated US$8,000 million.

Nationally the picture is not much better. It doesn't take an expert to see that we need an injection of new capital to expand our commercial operations. One solution is to try and attract investors who are willing, under current conditions, to open businesses inside the country. That is far from easy since the US tightened its embargo by passing the Cuban Democracy Act (the 'Torricelli Law') in 1992. While Cuba had the Council of Mutual Economic Assistance to support it, the US embargo could be ignored. Official figures show, however, that that embargo has cost the country more than US$41,000 million in lost trade since 1962.

The idea is that a flood of new investors will have a multiplying effect on production, on exports and on local consumption. So far, however, the level of new investment has not been enough to offset the general shortages of resources of all kinds, which set in at the start of the 1990s with Castro's so-called 'special period' of economic retrenchment. Furthermore, this period has marked the breakdown of many of the social successes that we had previously achieved, although it has been possible to maintain others.

Before 1959, the general illiteracy rate was 23.6 per cent, reaching 41.7 per cent among the rural population. The average level of schooling was something below third grade, with only around 6 per cent of children who matriculated in state schools getting as far as the sixth grade. And only 45 per cent of children of school age actually matriculated in the first place. These levels were greatly improved by a successful educational policy, but now they are beginning to slide back: it is hard to maintain attendance rates when pupils don't have shoes, or uniforms, or even the guarantee of a decent breakfast at home or a packed lunch to take to school.

Many of the Secondary Schools and Pre-University Institutes (ESBEC-IPUEC) have closed, some of them converted into housing or into government offices. Also, many teachers have gone into exile. The policy aim of producing more university graduates has led to many being subsequently unable to find suitable jobs, while others go into academic careers that are less than useful for solving the developmental problems we face: degrees in Marxist-Leninist philosophy, for example...

There are similar problems with the health system. This guarantees universal access to free medical care. In 1950, the average life expectancy was 62.3 years; now it is 75.5 years. In 1958, the infant mortality rate stood at 40 per 1,000 live births; now it is down to 9.4. In 1959 the ratio of women dying in childbirth was 118.2 per 100,000; that has been reduced to 26.9. Other indicators, however, reflect the food shortage, worsening living conditions and poor sanitation, such as the increase in low birthweight babies from 7.3 per cent in 1989 to 9 per cent in 1993. Viral infections, such as hepatitis, are on the increase, along with scabies and other ailments linked to poor personal hygiene caused by the shortage of soap and detergent.

Meanwhile, around 80 per cent of our industrial capacity has been lost because of the scarcity of raw materials, fuel and other resources. Those industries that still operate desperately need to rationalise their staffing levels. Central to the ideal of the perfect society was the establishment of full employment. This ambition has been directly responsible for one of the most serious elements in the present crisis. Our factories have been crammed with workers: where one was needed, they put in three or four. It didn't matter, the state would take responsibility. The lack of any incentives to increase productivity has had a disastrous effect on workers' attitudes towards their jobs. ➤

NÉSTOR BAGUER
Health for hard currency

The National Health System, which has brought expert medical care to the remotest parts of the country, is the pride of the Cuban Revolution. The skill of its doctors is beyond dispute, but with the current shortages of vital medical equipment and supplies they can no longer do a proper job.

Not so long ago, at the age of 73, I broke my hip. A couple of friends took me to the nearest hospital, La Benéfica. My first impression was horrendous: poorly lit corridors, filthy floors and walls, even the occasional cockroach. Nonetheless, I was dealt with promptly: an x-ray was taken, I saw a specialist. He told me I needed an operation to set the bone but because the operating theatre wasn't sterile, they couldn't treat me there. An ambulance was called to take me the Frank País Hospital, just outside Havana. I was in a lot of pain, so asked for a painkilling injection. The doctor looked at me rather wistfully and said: 'I'm very sorry, but we don't even have aspirin here.'

Fortunately the ambulance soon arrived, and a few minutes later I was at the Frank País. What a difference! Beautiful buildings surrounded by pretty gardens, gleaming corridors, nurses who came running to my room at once to give me a sedative, while the analyst took a blood sample to determine my blood group. Then the registrar arrived to check my medical history and, finally, the orthopaedic surgeon. He confirmed the diagnosis from the x-ray, and scheduled me in for an operation the following morning. Everything went like clockwork. The following morning, I was taken back to my room, and four days later, after excellent attention throughout my stay, I was discharged.

There are a couple of reasons for the marked difference between the two hospitals. The Frank País has a source of income from the many foreigners who are drawn to Cuba by the reputation of its specialists. With hard currency it can obtain supplies on the international market, to which other hospitals don't have access. Most people have to make do with hospitals like the Benéfica.

But it's also a case of administrative inefficiency. Even in the best hospitals, patients have to provide their own soap, towels, a glass to drink from, cutlery and so forth, which have all disappeared. The dirt in the Benéfica's corridors and operating theatres doesn't need dollars to wash it away: it was totally renovated just a few years ago. If the administrators took more pride in their work, then perhaps, despite the shortages, they could provide a better service to the people. ❑

For instance, in the country's major income generator, the sugar industry, the last three years have seen a steady drop in production. The most recent harvest, for which there are as yet no official figures, is estimated at 3.2 million tons, making it one of the smallest yields in the last 50 years. The government is talking of a 'sugar recovery' in 1996, on the basis of recently secured financial loans — made under very stringent conditions — that have facilitated the purchase of fertilisers, pesticides and herbicides. The central sugar refiners don't grind money, however, but sugar cane. And that is produced by people, the same people who lack any proper incentive to increase their productivity.

The standard of living has declined dramatically during the 'special period'. The monthly food ration, which is actually only enough for about 10 days, goes down all the time, forcing people to supplement their supplies from the Farmers' Market, or on the black market. For that, people have to change their Cuban pesos into US dollars. This reduces the buying power of the peso, which effectively reduces the average wage. Family life becomes ever harder: the adults have to spend most of their spare time out on the streets, trying to get some extra food or other basic necessities, while the younger generation have scarely any opportunities for recreational or creative pursuits.

The people are highly adaptable, and have been tightening their belts day by day, but the effect of living this way is to destroy any hope of ever having a better future.

Although everyone knows that poverty, unemployment and social disintegration have structural causes, there is no political will to attempt a redefinition of the prevailing model of socio-economic development. On the contrary, the search is on for reforms that will leave the centralised state intact. However, some of the measures that have been taken have opened a chink in the wall, especially the authorisation of the Farmers' Market which has sown the seed of a system of free supply and demand. It has also given a degree of official recognition to an already existing social group: the *macetas* [misers], the name given to people who manage to accumulate vast amounts of money. For many people who have found it hard to get a steady supply of food, perhaps the Farmers' Market offers a form of security because, although the prices are out of the reach of some, at least the products are there, waiting for those who can afford them. But for the average worker, with a wage of 188 pesos per month, it isn't of great help considering that a pound of pork costs between 35 and

40 pesos, a pound of rice or beans between 10 and 12 pesos.

The government has tried to improve the unemployment problem by extending the opportunities for self-employment. However, the 150 or so authorised private businesses have not been as successful as was hoped. This is mainly because many of these businesses require raw materials and equipment which the state does not supply. A recent measure, to authorise the establishment of small restaurants, has proved impracticable because food producers are demanding payment in hard currency. Still, the demand for enterprise permits heavily outstrips supply: around 170,000 people have applied for permission to start a small business.

The new economic policy has also been aimed at concentrating investment in sectors which are quick to make returns, especially international tourism. Fifteen years ago, this didn't enter into the country's development plans. In a relatively short period, tourism has become the second biggest generator of convertible currency, behind the sugar industry, with an annual growth rate, from 1988 to 1993, of 12 per cent (albeit from a base level of zero). Over the last several years, the number of hotel rooms has risen by an average of 3,000 each year.

Some 60 per cent of the Caribbean holiday market — the amount accounted for by US tourists — is closed to us by the US embargo, which also therefore greatly limits the possibilities for further growth in this sector. Growth potential is also limited by internal factors, such as the crumbling infrastructure, which hampers the development of other tourist services, aside from hotels.

Meanwhile, the arrival of ever greater numbers of tourists has led to a rise in the number of prostitutes, known here as *jiniteras*, a social problem that had been successfully contained for more than 25 years; just as the *aceritos* [street children], aged between 6 and 13, who swarm round tourists to ask them for change, have begun to appear again.

But hope remains that present economic reforms in the direction of the free market will go further and will coalesce into a much-needed overhaul of the prevailing socio-economic model. The danger is, though, that the longer we wait for that to happen, the more likely we are to lose our hard-won social achievements. ❑

Marta Beatriz Roque Cabello is vice-president of the National Association of Independent Cuban Economists (ANEIC) in Havana

RICARDO REY DE LEÓN
Thou shalt respect thy President — and all his works

The state has numerous ways of dealing with those who express their disagreement with the regime. Among the most widely used of these is the crime of *desacato* (disrespect).

Chapter II of the Cuban Penal Code, 'Violence, Disobedience and Causing Offence to Authorities, Public Functionaries and their Agents', gives a broad definition of *desacato* under Section 3 Article 144, paragraphs 1 and 2:

1. Whoever threatens, defames, maligns, injures and in any way insults or offends, orally or in writing, the dignity or propriety of any authority, public official, or any of their auxiliary agents, with regard to the exercise of their duties or in the execution of those same duties, shall be punished by loss of liberty for between three months and one year, or a fine of between 100 and 300 pesos, or both.

2. If the offence set out in the previous paragraph is committed against the President of the Council of State, the President of the National Assembly of Popular Power, or against the members of the Council of State or of the Council of Ministers, or against Deputies to the National Assembly of Popular Power, the punishment shall be loss of liberty for between one and three years.

Unlike political offences such as enemy propaganda and clandestine printing, also used against dissenters, *desacato* is a common crime.

Historically, when Cubans disagreed with their rulers, they would subject them to fierce popular criticism: political satire and ridicule were central characteristics of the national sense of humour.

Prior to the Revolution, the mass media were the platform for satire. Since their replacement by the offence of *desacato*, many humourists have disappeared from the scene, their place taken by graffiti in public places, one of the few ways still left for voicing opposition to the state. It, too, is punishable under the *desacato* ordinance. And before the court passes sentence, those apprehended will have been subjected to exactly the same repressive investigation and trial usually reserved for counter-revolutionary political activists. They too will serve their time alongside common criminals of all kinds, treated as just another *compañero*. ❑

Ricardo Rey De León is an independent lawyer based in Havana

NÉSTOR BAGUER

In search of an ethic

Cuban journalism has a long independent, democratic tradition. From the eighteenth century, when the first Cuban newspaper was published under the title *Diario del Apostadero* (Daily Post), the influence and authority of the press grew rapidly. Today, incompetence is as great a threat as censorship

During the War of Independence (1895-1898), *Patria*, the paper founded by José Martí, was in the vanguard of the struggle for freedom. At the turn of this century, with independence from Spain won, newspapers sprang up all over the island. The conservative *Diario de la Marina* was followed by *El Mundo*, *La Discusión*, *La Lucha*, *Havana Post*, *PM* and dozens more. In Havana alone, there were some 15 dailies and six weekly magazines.

By the 1950s, Cuba was producing papers of exceptionally high professional quality for a small island with only five million inhabitants. Only two publications throughout the rest of Spanish America could compare: *La Prensa* in Buenos Aires and *Excelsior* in Mexico City.

The new revolutionary government showed immediate hostility to the press. The privately-owned newspaper *Alerta* was taken over — with no compensation to the owners — and relaunched as the daily *Revolución*, a mouthpiece of Fidel Castro's 26 July Movement. The next move instituted a system of prior censorship through the official union. All edited copy had to be submitted for vetting: after each edited paragraph, the union would add its own version, always contradicting what the original had said.

In 1965, the government merged *Revolución* with the Communist Party's publication *Noticias de Hoy* (The News Today) and named the new paper *Granma*, after the boat that carried the first guerrillas to Cuba from exile in Mexico. In place of the evening papers came *Juventud Rebelde* (Rebel Youth), the organ of the young Communists, and *Trabajadores* (Workers), published by the Central Workers' Union.

At the same time, municipal and provincial papers were disappearing, leaving only a few under new names, all of them completely controlled by the Party. Only two magazines survived: *Mujeres* (Women) and *Bohemia*, along with the newly created propaganda publication *Cuba*, for circulation overseas.

As a result of all this, the most capable and experienced media professionals went into exile, including most of the teachers at Havana's School of Journalism. The school finally shut its doors when the government refused to recognise the academic qualifications it bestowed. This obliged the few graduates who had remained in the country to repeat their professional education at the Party's own journalism school.

With the vast majority of teachers in exile, the government was forced to improvise. The replacement teachers lacked the necessary professional experience and the curriculum was poor. The inadequacy of the new graduates was increasingly demonstrated by the monumental errors of

News-stand Havana 1995: *many languages, but a single voice*

grammar, lack of style and ignorance of the plain facts of Cuban history evident in their work on radio, TV and in the press.

Today Cuba has no editorial writers, columnists or sub-editors who are dedicated to maintaining proper professional standards. The creativity, the sense of investigation, the pursuit of the facts behind events, the sense of performing an honest service in informing the public, have all been lost. Even worse, any sense of professional ethics has long gone. It is not enough for a journalist simply to accept that he is denied entry to a factory where there are rumours of corruption or bad work practices; and to publish the official line verbatim, without protesting at the lack of access, or refusing to publish information which is riddled with falsehoods.

What kind of journalism is it, when the radio news bulletins are simply read out from the day's edition of *Granma*? What kind of journalism is it, when you can read exactly the same information, whether you're looking at *Granma, Juventud Rebelde* or *Trabajadores*? Even Fidel Castro pointed out, at a congress of the official Cuban Journalists' Union (UPEC) that, if *Granma* publishes a communiqué from the Ministry for Foreign Relations on the first page, top left-hand corner, then there it will be in the other papers too, same place, same point size and all. Of course no-one dares to offer any commentary on the information they reproduce.

This is not simply a matter of official censorship. In the majority of cases, it is a combination of self-censorship and incompetence, inspired by a fear of losing one's job, one's car, the trips abroad and so on. My personal experience of working in the various communications media taught me how it is. When I touched on prickly subjects, expressed an opinion that contradicted the opinions of officials, they often warned me to be more careful.

Instead of defending the rights of journalists, UPEC, the official union, was simply an instrument of the government and did nothing to defend its members. In 1988, the Association of Independent Cuban Journalists (APIC), was formed to fight for a free and democratic press, for freedom and respect for the profession, for decent pay and conditions and, above all, for ethics, competence and professional pride. ❑

Néstor Baguer worked with Radio Havana for many years and is now president of the Association of Independent Cuban Journalists (APIC)

YNDAMIRO RESTANO DÍAZ
Poem

I AM a creative mirror:
And my existence
Relies on these things:
Rat
River
Intellect
Death
The absence of the crowd;
The whole mixed up with particular things
The self-creative void,
Alone and self-contained,
Trying to sigh with the lake.

I AM the creative mirror:
The great wise image,
Covered in smoke,
Which opens a path between the steam and flames
To tell you: have faith,
Be free, love.

Yndamiro Restano Díaz *was arrested in December 1991 and sentenced to 10 years in prison for 'rebellion' over his activities with the independent protest movement Armonía (Harmony), which he founded in 1990. He also founded the Association of Independent Cuban Journalists (APIC). After his unexpected release on 1 June 1995, Yndamiro Restano visited London. He believes his release was 'a gesture' by the government, in the hope of gaining trade concessions from the West. He was assured that he and others will be permitted to work independently in Cuba. While he was in London, however, reports came through from Cuba of the harassment or detention of several independent journalists, among them Néstor Baguer (see page 129, 133). Nonetheless, Restano plans to return to Cuba in August and set up a small independent newspaper, called* Armonía

Poem translated by Mandy Garner
Translation supported by funding from the Arts Council of England

GUSTAVO ARCOS BERGNES

Whose army?

Fidel Castro's former comrade-in-arms talks to Adam Newey of the repression of dissidents and his hope for a peaceful transition to democracy with the help of the army

AN: *In his book* Mea Cuba, *Guillermo Cabrera Infante refers to you as 'the reluctant hero' and 'a genuine hero of the Revolution'. But wasn't your relationship to the armed struggle always ambivalent, to say the least?*

GAB: I wasn't fighting for the imposition of a Communist regime in Cuba, but for the restoration of the 1940 Constitution and against the military regime of Batista.

The different groups who fought against Batista's dictatorship agreed on a number of things: to set up a provisional government for 18 months and then to re-establish the Constitution of 1940, as well as bring in certain necessary complementary laws (for example, agrarian reform), along western lines. And also to establish a tribunal of accounts to prevent the corruption that had gone on under successive governments. After those 18 months there were to be elections, with free participation of political parties every four years.

The authors of the 1940 Constitution prohibited presidential re-election for two consecutive terms. With Castro in charge it has been completely different. His regime is endless. He has been in power for 36 years, running a completely totalitarian system of government.

You knew Castro personally: you fought with him in the Moncada assault in July 1953, the first armed rising against Batista, and you subsequently spent time with him in prison. What kind of a man is he?

I'm 68 years old, and I can tell you a man is many things, something indefinable. Fidel Castro is at the end of his political life, perhaps of his physical life as well and I'm reminded of something a Russian writer said of a supreme egotist: 'He had only one great and abiding love in his life — his own self.'

When, sometime in the future, historians describe the period from 1959 up till — who knows when — it will not be the history of Cuba they tell, but the story of one man: Fidel Castro.

Tell me about the work of your organisation, the Cuban Committee for Human Rights (CCPDH).

The CCPDH was the first organisation to struggle for the peaceful restoration of human rights in Cuba. Not just social and economic rights, but civil and political rights too. Its founder, in the late 1970s, was Ricardo Bofill [*Index* 6/1984], today living in exile in the United States. Throughout the '80s, people who felt excluded by the Communist system but repudiated all forms of violent opposition joined us. The majority of the population is confused but still believes in the wisdom and honesty of Castro as a ruler. Castro's propaganda convinced them that any Cuban who had some disagreement with the government or with him personally was a traitor, an agent of the Yankee government. The authorities also attacked our private lives, alleging every sin in the book.

Abroad, many honest people — politicians, intellectuals, press — still looked on Castro's government, as we say, 'with good eyes'. The excesses were already known in the West but were in part justified by many on the grounds that Castro was trying to establish a higher form of justice.

Over the last year there seems to have been a modicum of liberalisation. The acts of repudiation have stopped, there is greater toleration of gays, the church is becoming a little stronger. Why is Castro loosening his grip?

He has to. Since losing the support of the Soviet Union, the regime is totally without resources, without credit among western countries, without hard currency. In July 1993 he had to go ahead with the 'dollarisation' of the economy and was forced to accept certain humanitarian measures in civilian and political life.

But he still maintains, perhaps with more subtlety, a repressive system against the dissidents: for example, my brother [Sebastián Arcos], Yndamiro Restano [both subsequently released on 1 June 1995], many others. Especially in the provinces, in the interior; here in Havana, an agglomeration of 2 million people, everything that happens is under the eye of the diplomatic corps and the foreign press agencies. In a sense, the regime is obliged to accept the relationship between the West and our movement. What you are doing now was unthinkable until the late '70s. Thanks to the efforts made by the dissidents and by our compatriots in exile and international organisations — especially the UN's annual sessions in Geneva — the Cuban government has been condemned this year, for the fourth successive time, as a systematic violator of human rights.

Last November, the UN's human rights commissioner, Jorge Ayala Lasso, was allowed to visit Cuba for the first time, but his visit was far from satisfactory. It was too short, the contact with representatives of the human rights groups and dissidents in general was too meagre. He had no contact at all with political prisoners or their families, he didn't visit the provinces. In the three days in which he was in Cuba he limited himself to meetings with Castro, the ministers of the interior and justice and other representatives of the government.

Was it a complete waste of time, or did the visit at least have some symbolic significance?

Symbolic, yes. But as far as the Cuban people are concerned, it was a deception: they expected something rather different. At the end of his visit he was interviewed by the press — not the Cuban press, which has its hands over its mouth — but the foreign press accredited in Cuba. They asked him what he had asked from Castro's regime. Two things, he replied: first, that the Cuban government sign the various accords and agreements approved and accepted by the majority of the member states of the UN on the abolition of all forms of torture, physical and psychological, against political prisoners. The government promised to study his request 'favourably'. Second, that the government release a number of political prisoners. Not a general amnesty, simply special treatment for a few people. According to Mr Ayala Lasso, the government promised to study his list 'most favourably'. In the months since his visit, some political prisoners have indeed been released, but only on the condition that they leave the country, so it weakens the opposition here.

You said earlier that Castro is coming to the end of his political life, that reform must come soon. What form will that take? Will it be primarily economic? Can there be real political change?

Political change is indispensable. Castro must disappear in Cuba if we are to return to a representative government with full powers and all the fundamental liberties. After all the suffering here, the thousands in exile, dissidents imprisoned, a constitution will be necessary to enshrine rights and freedoms in law. We need a regime in which human rights, civil and political, social and economic, will be respected at the same level.

One thing Castro could do to take the pressure off himself is to take steps — as in China — to liberalise the economy and alleviate some of the suffering, without worrying at all about political freedom.

I'm no economist, but the superficial changes — for example, seeking inward investment in Cuba, creating mixed corporations with private and public capital, and now in the agricultural sector giving the use of state farms to private groups, to farmers, but only because of the necessity of the critical food shortages — don't seem to me to solve the fundamental problems of this country. In great measure these are to do with Fidel himself. He is like some great obstacle. Countries like China begin with liberalising the economy and later perhaps, as in the case of North Korea, with the disappearance of the doyen of the dictatorship, it is possible that a new leader, a new generation will initiate change. Deng Xiaoping is now a very old man and when he disappears from the political stage new generations of Chinese, building on existing developments, will change the totalitarian, repressive aspects of the

Communist system. The same will happen here in Cuba.

We dissidents put our trust in dialogue, in words rather than violence. There will be a change, and a transitional regime leading to democracy jointly managed by a new generation of civilians and military. And it must be achieved without violence or vengeance. Government representatives, *sotto voce*, are already admitting the necessity of such reforms. They know the antipathy of the population to government. They know that every Cuban family, even the highest in the land, is divided, has suffered the consequences of this system.

For over a year now, as a result of the new defence law, many key positions have been in the hands of either retired military or active military personnel. When the change comes, this will prevent it being accompanied by riots or the thirst for revenge. By all the laws of history, the army should be the most faithful defender of the new democratic republic. No two cases are ever exactly alike but, as in eastern Europe and in Nicaragua after the Sandinistas lost the elections, I see the army averting civil war, paving the way for a civilian government.

Perhaps the experience of Chile is instructive?

Like Chile, yes. The restoration of democracy in Chile was guaranteed by the army, which was powerful enough to prevent acts of vengeance against them. In Argentina, under the democratic governments of Alfonsín and Menem, the army has maintained order against all kinds of extremist movements. Let's hope that in Guatemala too, the president, who after all is the former human rights ombudsman, can maintain the peaceful transition to democracy now that the civil war is over.

We are optimists. I can't predict the future: I don't have the powers of a Nostradamus. But we think our optimism will be justified. ❑

Gustavo Arcos Bergnes *was Cuba's ambassador to Belgium from 1959-1964. He spent three years in prison in the late 1960s for unspecified crimes against the state, and in 1982 was sentenced, together with his brother Sebastián, to 14 years for attempting to leave the country illegally. He is currently president of the Cuban Committee for Human Rights (CCPDH) in Havana*

ALBERTO ABREU ARCIA

Memory of a punishment

He's locked me up again, and I don't know what is better; being out there, or being here in a corner of the room with bottle tops digging into my knees, scanning the wall for some point where my eyes can rest to relieve my fatigue.

From here I can see the rain falling on the house. (The house is a vast lagoon surrounded by monsters and gigantic ants.) Granny nods off in her chair, oblivious to the birdshit falling on her head from the roof and to uncle's absence; he's been shut away in his room for about an hour trying on the hats and dresses that she wore when she was a girl. And I wet myself laughing when I saw him wiggling his hips in front of the mirror. I look at him and laugh, I choke with laughter. Shit, I've never laughed so much. Not even that afternoon when the flying dogs and rattlesnakes appeared. I ran to warn them all, but they didn't believe me. Not even He did; He who now looks so nervous, pacing from one side of the house to the other, His face so contorted with frowning that it almost hides — behind the innumerable wrinkles that plough his forehead — those two crystal balls filled with blood. It's the alcohol that makes Him swear, that makes Him say how could a son of mine have turned out like this... Today is the ninth day — counting every second of every hour — that it has rained without stopping. The puddles around the house are lagoons, rats' nests, where the huge snakes come from.

It is time to grab granny's wrist and ask her softly: shall we do dirty stuff? Without anyone else hearing. The way He says to my mother: shall we do dirty stuff? And she fidgets nervously, smiles, and glances surreptitiously in all directions. Shall we do dirty stuff? Until granny arrives and she threatens to tell her everything.... Every time He returns, the same thing happens; playing finishes, wailing begins, his dry voice like thunder shitting on my grandmother, my mother's dead mother, who starts to shout, to scream that she won't take any more, that she'll up and leave when we least expect it. He looks at her and says accusingly: it can't be true that a son of mine has turned out like this. Then He comes to the room and turns on the light. I look at Him out of the corner of my eye, He stops in front of me; He knows I'm watching Him, that I can see Him in profile; but He stays there as if He had decided never to move again. You're a disgrace, if you carry on like this you'll end up like your uncle. It'd be better if you'd never been born, He says. Then He walks away, reeling around as if all the walls in the world couldn't hold him. I don't care any more, you could lock me up for a hundred nights; to make you a man. One hundred nights locked up in the dark room. This is the first night and it hasn't stopped raining. It's almost nine months — counting every hour of every day — since it started raining, threatening to completely flood the house; I'm the only one who knows it, and if He weren't punishing me, if I hadn't been put here, to repent, I would go and warn them: leave now. We have to run away because soon there'll be no escape. My mother, who has just realised, has run out. Her lips pressed tightly together, her hair in tufts like lengths of rope dangling down her face, saying over and over again that she won't put up with it any more, that she'll up and leave if He hits her again; she is pursued by the screams of my grandmother; she says she won't put up with this punishment for much longer either. Only uncle... Heaven, disappoint me. Tell me: what happened to my fantasy while I slept that I could have ended up in here ... carries on reading, or rather chewing the words he swallows and breathes out monotonously and with a tiredness that comes from an unknown recess of the soul.

He catches up with my mother, drags her home in the rain.

I remember the afternoon when I heard them arguing about uncle. He said He didn't want anything to do with him, and granny replied; he's your brother... I dream I am here, afflicted with this imprisonment, and I once dreamt that I was in happier surroundings... Better never to have been born. But it's not Him, it's not granny, or my uncle, but the people from round where I live, with their whispering and their grinning. The ones who say my uncle is effeminate. Lies — shouts granny as if she wished no-one would ever mention these things to her. But He just laughs.

My mother hasn't stopped crying.

I can't remember anything any more. I can only hear my granny's shouts, calling for Him, begging Him on her knees to leave me alone. But He doesn't answer, He thinks He's doing it for my own good, because otherwise I'll turn out like uncle... and the dark room is no longer dark because He has switched the light on, He comes over to me flicking his belt, making it dance around His shoulders, filling the room with threats, along with the shouts and pleas of my mother and grandmother imploring Him to leave me alone. And the distant voice, like a whisper, of my uncle...Shadows, a vision, and the greatest pleasure is small; life is a dream and dreams are but dreams...I look at His profile; you'll end up like your uncle, he says. Then I feel the first blows — but I'll kill you first. Like a dog.

Granny has started shouting again. She is calling Him, begging Him to come quickly because my mother is burning herself; but He isn't listening. Rain is flooding the house. While the belt flashes back and forth through the air I try to keep my eyes on His profile. Soon, the snakes and the ants will arrive, and together with the rain, they will flood through the house. ❑

Alberto Abreu Arcia *is one of the new generation of young Cuban writers known as the Novísimos*
Translated by Tom Nicholls
Translation supported by funding from the Arts Council of England

ARIEL HIDALGO

Miami vices

Hard-line exile groups in Miami maintain a firm grip over Washington's policy towards Cuba. Amid the clamour for tighter sanctions against Castro, the more moderate voices among the exile community cannot make themselves heard

On my very first day in Miami in 1988, fresh from a Cuban prison, I found myself standing in front of a radio set. I was tremendously curious: whose were these voices coming from the speaker? I remembered the propaganda programmes on Cuba's official radio stations, the tendentious news and hysterical spite-filled allegations about 'imperialist lackeys'. And now here I was, in a supposedly free society, listening to someone hurling abuse at supposed 'turncoats' and 'Communist infiltrators'.

I was stunned. If you changed just a few of the phrases it could have come straight off Radio Rebelde, one of the Castroist stations in Havana. On a visit to Miami in 1995, Cuba's Cardinal Jaime Ortega summed up the similarity in six words: 'The same coin, with two sides'. Others have described the most powerful sector of the exile community here simply as 'Castroism in reverse'.

For this sector, everything boils down to a Manichaean opposition between Communists and anti-Communists which can only be resolved by bloodshed. Some broadcasters, those who cry out for war with Cuba, even present their radio programmes dressed in camouflage. The closest to battle most exiles have come, however, is trying to get served in the coffee bars along Miami's Calle Ocho.

There are others who don't talk of war as such, but promote it indirectly by advocating a tightening of the embargo, to reduce Cuba to starvation in the belief that hunger will force people out onto the streets to face the tanks. Anyone who puts forward other views about how to bring democracy to Cuba is branded an 'infiltrator', a covert agent of

Castroism. Just as in Cuba, anyone who deviates from the Party line is branded an 'agent of imperialism'.

Such images as these fix the cliché of the Cuban exile community as a bunch of ultra-right-wing terrorists. But in fact that picture represents only a tiny segment of the diaspora. The rest, the vast majority, either stay silent or they cover up their real opinions — just as they would have to in Cuba — for fear of losing their jobs or being publicly reviled. According to some acute observers, however, what is now happening in Miami is the result of a backlash by that small but influential sector of the community who feel threatened by the realisation that the tide of history is turning decisively away from them.

Soon after my arrival in 1988, I came across a number of exiles who were considered socialists or anarchists. Some organisations, like Democratic Independent Cuba, formed by Húber Matos, one of the guerrilla leaders who fought against Batista, maintained a truly democratic line and respected divergent opinions. Others, those pejoratively referred to as *dialogueras,* that mainly came to prominence at the beginning of the 1990s, advocate a policy of dialogue and reconciliation with the Cuban government. These include the Democratic Platform, a coalition of parties comprising liberals, social democrats and Christian democrats; the Cuban Committee for Democracy (CCD), composed principally of academics, professionals and business people; and the group Cambio Cubano [Cuban Change], led by the former guerrilla leader Eloy Gutiérrez Menoyo.

None of these people are recent exiles, but old campaigners with huge experience among the diaspora. The two successive presidents of the CCD, Marcelino Miyares and Alfredo Durán, were part of the expeditionary force that landed at the Bay of Pigs in 1961 and were promptly defeated at Girón; Gutiérrez Menoyo fled Cuba in the first years of the Revolution and was captured in 1965, disembarking in Cuba with a group of armed men, for which he spent 21 years in prison.

Since the end of the Cold War and the demise of the Eastern European regimes, these men have moderated their views. Furthermore, the various waves of Cuban migration, first from the port of Mariel in 1980, and then more sporadically in the years that followed, made up principally of dissidents from different spheres in society, have, little by little, been generating a groundswell of more realistic opinion in Miami. The new mentality strays ever further from the traditional hard line of the main power groups that control most of the important media.

For many years these media actively encouraged Cubans to board their rafts and attempt the almost suicidal crossing of the Straits of Florida, treating anyone who fled the island as a hero and as living proof of the desperate situation created by the Castroist administration. In mid-1994, the number of rafters increased dramatically. However, rather than diminishing, the number of people arriving on the Florida coast reached a thousand a day, severely embarrassing the US government.

Immediately the voices on exile stations began their clamour: 'Clinton, don't allow another Mariel!', 'Clinton, don't let Castro dictate this country's immigration policy!' Then the powerful Cuban-American National Foundation weighed in. According to a press release put out by the Foundation, Jorge Mas Canosa, the Foundation's president, proposed a series of measures during a meeting with Clinton 'designed to resolve the crisis created by the regime of Fidel Castro in Cuba'. Hours later, on 18 August, it was announced that thousands of rafters would be sent back from Florida to the US naval base in Cuba at Guantánamo Bay, that the number of charter flights between the two countries would be reduced, and that exiles would no longer be permitted to send US dollars to friends and families in Cuba.

To the great surprise of the Foundation's leaders, however, the exiles were having none of it. There was immediate criticism of the new measures. Clinton was violating the rights of those fleeing the Communist hell. The camps at Guantánamo were compared with Nazi concentration camps. Practically no-one, meanwhile, chose to remember the political prisoners locked up in altogether more dramatic fashion in Cuba, or the opposition activists harassed in the streets by government agents. And while dissidents in Cuba had to give up their political activities in order to concentrate on finding the basic necessities of life after the supply of dollars from their friends and families on the outside dried up, exile groups were organising collections for the 30,000 internees at Guantánamo. Some people even began to criticise the Foundation in public.

Mas Canosa rushed to declare that the Guantánamo decision was nothing to do with him and that the Foundation was taking steps to get the Guantánamo rafters admitted into the United States, making the Clinton administration the target for criticism which extended as far as Geneva. People such as the former US ambassador to the United

Nations, Armando Valladares, who had kept silent over the Mariel exiles (some of whom were imprisoned for years under successive Republican administrations after completing their prison sentences) took the opportunity of venting all their indignation against the Democrats.

In the face of this criticism, and fearing that disturbances among Cuban rafters held at a US military base in Panama might also break out at Guantánamo, the Clinton administration held secret negotiations with the Cuban government and decided to admit the Guantánamo internees. To try and placate the powerful strand of anti-immigration opinion at home, however, they balanced this measure with a pledge to return to Cuba anyone found trying to reach the Florida coast from 2 May onwards. In effect, the policy of preferential entry for Cuban refugees fleeing the Communist tyranny, established by President Johnson, had been struck down.

No-one in Miami was especially grateful to the government for doing what they had been asking it to do for eight-and-a-half months, because they had already forgotten about the thousands of detained rafters and the supposed 'concentration camps'. By this time it was impossible to tune in to the exile radio stations without hearing hysterial cries of 'Traitor Clinton!' There was much talk about how the 'Cuban people's dream of freedom' was being denied, as if that dream consisted only in emigrating

CUBA: EXILES

to the United States. There were even declarations of war against the Yankees, and several groups proclaimed a campaign of Martin Luther King-style civil disobedience. Freeways were blocked by protesters, bringing traffic to a halt, and demonstrations were organised. The number of participants, however, in a city with a Cuban population of over 800,000, was always much lower than expected.

But it wasn't the fate of future rafters that worried the exile leaders so much, however, as the thought of those secret meetings, the possibility that the two governments might hammer out their differences behind their backs, and lift the economic embargo. For a mindset that cannot conceive of a resolution of the Cuban drama without a US presence, that scenario would signify the definitive collapse of the anti-Castroist cause.

In the world at large, however, the winds are blowing in other directions: the secretary-general of the Organisation of American States (OAS), César Gaviria, has argued strongly in favour of Cuba's readmittance to that body. The dissident Elizardo Sánchez has issued a public invitation to former US president, Jimmy Carter, to visit the island. Two civic leaders, Sebastián Arcos and Yndamiro Restano, released from prison in June thanks to the efforts of the humanitarian group France Liberté, have issued messages urging reconciliation. On 15 June this year the group Diálogo Interamericano organised a visit for former Latin American presidents, among them the Nobel laureate Oscar Arias of Costa Rica, the architect of the Esquipulas Accords that ended the war in Nicaragua, to talk to government representatives and dissidents in Cuba. On a tour of exile communities in Miami and New Jersey, Cardinal Ortega brought his message of reconciliation among all Cubans. And in Havana, the government has held talks with ex-Comandante Eloy Gutiérrez Menoyo.

After Yndamiro Restano mentioned the possibility of creating a social-democratic party in Cuba, all the radio stations in Miami were quick to dismiss it as a 'tyrannical manoeuvre' to set up a fictitious opposition in Cuba. The members of Diálogo Interamericano didn't escape the insults either, especially Oscar Arias, who was accused of trying to save his 'friend' Fidel Castro. That backfired, however, when Arias left Havana for Miami on 18 June, affirming that there was little political will for change in Cuba, where people were living in a police state. The same people who had recently vilified him were effusive in their praise. For Gutiérrez Menoyo, who has spent almost 40 years fighting for liberty in Cuba, they reserved their most unpleasant insults. And Cardinal Ortega, who 30 years ago suffered the torture of the forced labour camps and who bravely increased the standing and authority of the Catholic Church by condemning totalitarianism and the paramilitary 'rapid response brigades', could barely be heard preaching his sermon of love and reconciliation above the mob of hard-line exiles in the church shouting him down as an 'agent of Castro' and a 'whore' in an archetypically Castroist act of repudiation.

Not long ago a friend of mine, a journalist at the *Miami Herald*, said to me: 'For 40 years the people of Israel wandered through Sinai in search of the promised land. So far we've been wandering for 36.' I thought that the Sinai part of her analogy, at least, was apt, because if one thing is certain, it is that the exile community, with its outdated attitudes, has condemned itself to wandering all alone in the world. And so it will continue, for far longer than 40 years, until we understand that freedom isn't won by simply crossing a border; that we must search deep within ourselves to root out for ever the seeds of captivity that lurk there. ❑

Ariel Hidalgo *spent almost seven years in prison for 'enemy propaganda' and 'incitement against the social order'. He now runs the Human Rights Information Bureau in Miami*

JOSÉ CONRADO RODRÍGUEZ
Out of the lie

Open letter to Fidel Castro given as a sermon by the priest of the Iglesia del Rosario, in Palma Soriano, Oriente, Cuba

To Señor Fidel Castro Ruz, President of the Republic of Cuba

Dear Señor Presidente:

My deep preoccupation with the situation through which our people are now living moves me to write to you, in the hope that you might consider my concerns, and see fit to give them an answer.

Many ordinary people absolve you of blame because, they say, you don't know the truth of what is happening here. I cannot agree with them. How could you not know all about the wretched situation that afflicts almost 11 million Cubans on this island? I'm not going to try, therefore, to reveal to you a reality you already know, but to lead you to see that same reality from a new perspective.

Through more than 30 years, our country endorsed a politics whose cornerstone was violence, and whose justification was the presence, just 90 miles away, of a powerful and implacable enemy: the United States of America. The way we faced up to such a powerful enemy was by putting ourselves under the protection of the power that, for many years, was its rival: the Soviet Union. And so we joined the orbit of countries that made up the Socialist bloc, led by that superpower.

While the Soviet Union supported our economy massively and steadily, and gave decisive help to us in the arms race, Cuba was falling into a state of internal violence and profound repression. Abroad, we became embroiled in a series of conflicts that sucked us into the maelstrom of global violence. Through war and through propaganda we became protagonists, masters of confrontation throughout the world. But the politics of confrontation have become irrelevant, ineffectual, since the Soviet Union and the socialist bloc disappeared. For a while, it looked like an effective enough policy, but it turns out to have been misguided.

JOSÉ CONRADO RODRÍGUEZ

At home and abroad, the use of hatred and violence, of suspicion and enmity, have been the chief cause of our past and present misery.

Today we can see that more clearly than ever. A bloated state that grows ever more powerful left our people defenceless and silenced. The total absence of that space of liberty in which honest criticisms and alternative views can find a place, drew us down a perilous slope towards social and political intolerance. Its fruits were hypocrisy and deception, lies and insincerity, and a general state of intimidation that affected everyone on the island. Those policies have wrecked our economy; we have lost all sense of the value of things and, what's worse, the value of people. Violence and repression can lead only to contempt for human life. We aren't used to earning our bread with the sweat of our brows, but instead to a huge dependency on whatever help may be given us. We have been living a lie, deceived and self-deceiving. We have done wrong, and our wrongs have turned against us, have been visited upon us.

We are all responsible, but no-one more so than you. I've heard it said many times that even those closest to you fear you. I've heard it said that even your own children have been rebuffed when they have tried to tell you these truths. I know that this country's Catholic bishops have at least tried to reason with you on these subjects, but without being heard. I no longer wish to — nor, in conscience, can I — remain silent. For even now, I believe our course can be changed and our country — as you so often say is your wish — can be saved.

Right now, if you so wished, we could find a peaceful, negotiated settlement, one that comes from the very heart of our country, through a national dialogue that includes all the different tendencies within the Communist Party, the dissident groups within the country and, perhaps, even those Cubans in exile. We could put in train a process of free, popular, democratic consultation, which, in a climate of respect and tolerance, would allow the voice of our people to be heard. If you would lead that process, with respect for the purity of democratic judgement, it would avoid the bloodbath that the present state of affairs presages as our inevitable, miserable fate.

Those among our compatriots who still follow you would not refuse to take part in this process and keep it alive, as long as it comes from you. I'm certain that all the governments of the world, even those who are presently your adversaries; and I'm even more certain that all people of good faith, both here and abroad, will support such a step. But I'm fearful that if you don't take a decision soon, and in this spirit, then you will go down in the memory of our people — even of those who for years have been your followers — as the most disastrous ruler in Cuba's history.

On the other hand, the Cuban people are kind and good. They know how to be generous. They will recognise and be grateful that you have spared them the horrors of a civil war, or from the unnecessary prolongation of the present desperate state of our nation, and perhaps forget the injustices that have gone before. A long time ago, another Cuban priest, Padre Félix Varela, wrote these fine and wise words, whose meaning I now take fully as my own: 'When the motherland is in danger, when the insensible apathy of some, and the detestable treachery of others leads the sleepwalking populace towards the precipice: is it unwise to raise one's voice to warn of the impending danger? That is the wisdom of the weakling. My heart does not recognise it.'

In the name of the Lord, and in commending you to Our Lady of Charity [Cuba's patron saint], I beg you to accept these humble submissions of a poor priest, who shares with his people in their present anguish and their future hopes.

José Conrado Rodríguez, servant of Christ and of Cuba, 8 September 1994 ❑

DIARY

MÁRTON MESTERHÁZI

Journey to Bled

The European Broadcasting Union (EBU) holds meetings every two or three years for its radio drama experts, people who make radio plays in every form — from abstract sound to soap opera — for public service radio. The 1989 meeting, hosted by RAI, the Italian state broadcasting service, began in Florence the very weekend that the Berlin Wall came down. For broadcasters from eastern Europe things were about to change rapidly.

Márton Mersterházi of Magyar Radio made a plea from the heart at the final plenary. 'We drama people,' he said, 'have been allowed our little revolutions in the '70s when censorship gagged political plays. Censorship will vanish as economic crisis arrives.' There will be no money at that point, he went on, for the theatre, music, books or television. 'We radio people ought to become a last fortress of culture.' But where, he asked, will the money come from? Working from broken down studios and faced by commercial radio competition for the first time, managements were bound to follow policies of cheap, mass appeal programming. What was needed, he said, were not loans of millions of dollars but intellectual co-operation and support.

Shortly afterwards the EBU announced it had begun to work more closely with OIRT, the parallel organisation in eastern Europe. By the time of the next meeting, hosted by the BBC in Edinburgh in 1992, that co-operation was taking place against a background of fragmentation in the old political order in Russia and Yugoslavia and a bewildering rate of broadcasting change across the world.

The latest meeting took place in June, in Bled, hosted by RTV Slovenia, welcoming, for the first time, delegates from Russia, Estonia, Bulgaria, Poland, Slovakia, Macedonia and the radio stations of former East Germany. The problems of which Márton Mesterházi warned in 1989 had all become realities, evident to every delegate, whether from Australia or Canada, from eastern, western, northern, southern or central Europe. *Gillian Reynolds*

Diary

A proverbially beautiful alpine lake, a good hotel, well-organised evening programmes, and in the daytime the conference of radio-drama makers: a small, beleaguered army.

The new wall
Most conspicuous after the first day, it divides rich and poor more efficiently than the old one. Daniela and Dmitri find it impossible to pay US$500 to a foreign writer. (US$500 is a normal, decent fee.) They pay the 'equivalent' of US$25-100 to their own, in their stubbornly unconvertible eastern currencies. Marje-Mari's department has already had a 50 per cent staff reduction; now the new government wants to privatise all public broadcasting: 'it costs too much'.

The budget cuts
Some years ago, radio-play makers on the other side of the wall seemed to live in enviable comfort. Now the terror of the efficiency experts rages all over. John's department had its literary editors sacked, to make things cheaper and more popular. Stefan's department has had its budget withdrawn for overspending; staff reductions under way; he resigned. Martin's department had a 50 per cent staff reduction. Jane's management has decided no production team needs a literary or a music editor. Laurence's management wants to discipline drama by joining it to a super-department. Damiano's government has just agreed new, substantial budget cuts on national health, education, and culture.

Those efficiency experts, burning with neophyte ideological fervour, try to rehabilitate huge national economies with the tiny sums saved on the enemy territories of health, education and culture — mathematically absurd. Footnote: disgusting, too.

Technology
The difference between our two groups was most evident on the second day, devoted to digital technology. The formerly (and still quite) rich enthused, or raised warning fingers: digital technology is really wonderful, but it might debase the creative process into an assembly-line one and, in the hands of efficiency experts, will lead to further studio-time and personnel reductions. While we on the other side, did not even have to state the fact that our radios simply cannot afford such equipment, however sorely we might need it. Take the documentation of my department: it is still in 'The Book', a wardrobeful of stuffed envelopes and the memory of old colleagues.

'The dying species'
It struggles on heroically in absurd circumstances. Critical snobbery is one such: a novel or an art movie gets 10 times the attention of a radio play by the same author that reaches 10 times as many people. Still, the general atmosphere of naked fear was quite pungent at certain moments. The fear of able and competent people seeing the foreman with their sacks in his hands; getting offended, hurt, going on the defensive, developing various inferiority complexes, preaching old truths to each other and throwing home truths into the faces of powers that be — neither near nor interested.

If I look at how much leisure time US citizens waste a day on what rubbish, my heart feels the same sudden freeze.

In the face of all this we listened to the testimony of a blind Belgian listener, a 40-year-old lawyer, with a fine sense of humour, speaking ('Shpeaking/thpeaking') good English with a cleft palate. His job is giving legal aid to his blind compatriots; his hobby is listening to and recording radio plays from Belgium and the four countries around. He has recorded thousands of them, and has their documentation on his Braille-computer. He complains about radio drama getting scarcer, and more difficult to find, on account of insufficient slotting and information. But he believes in the future of the genre: people need real entertainment and recreation in this mad world.

Do I need to comment on this statement?

Let me, instead, give a description of a good radio-drama department. To provide listeners with novel and stage-play adaptations, radio plays for grown-ups and children, series, serials and soap, it would need minimally eight weekly slots on the different public radio channels. It would concentrate on good writing, old and new, from home and abroad, with a good proportion of the more 'entertaining genres'. It would be manned and funded to provide about 300 original broadcasts (the rest repeats) a

Slovenia 1995: the beauty of Bled

year, to commission its writers, translators, researcher-readers, actors and, occasionally, composers and musicians too. And it would do its best to avoid waste, to be cost effective.

The programmes of such a radio-drama department would naturally have minority audiences; important ones, though, which would otherwise die of spiritual scurvy. As soon as the terror of ideology-obsessed culture-haters finds a government alternative, funds may be re-channelled — public TV is a much better place to stage plays than radio.

Adapt or fight

The said alternative does not seem to be round the corner. What can the beleaguered army do now?

On opening the conference, the cultural minister of Slovenia states: his government has no intention of risking Slovenian culture; it wants to protect it as part of the nation's future; so, instead of withdrawal, they maintain state budget participation, even dominance, in that field. However, this most venerable (and for a Hungarian, enviable) striving of nineteenth century patriotism does not seem to be workable in the long run. And some colleagues told me later the statement has to be taken with a pinch of salt.

Anyhow, the beleaguered army has no nineteenth-century patriots to protect it.

One option is to fight. As so many of the offended, hurt people, defying their fear, said: fight the bosses for programme promotion and budgeting, re-educate station-managers, attract — as *new* listeners — the managing directors of your radio, the distributors of your public money, argue, convince, demonstrate, get allies within and outside the radio.

The other option, most articulately expounded by Damiano, is to adapt. He hates the terror of neophyte efficiency but considers it long range: not weather but climate. Better learn to live with it, accept the budget and personnel cuts to save the workshop and the genre, and prove to the 'experts' in their own language that you can be both efficient and popular; remember that radio drama has more enemies within the broadcasting industry than outside, so organise visibility (and solidarity for occasional resistance) in the TV, in the press, in other departments of the radio.

The two are not diametrically opposed. And both end with the same piece of advice, the common commandment of the small, beleaguered army of radio-play makers: make good programmes you believe in. ❏

Márton Mesterházi is a drama producer with Magyar Radio
Gillian Reynolds is radio critic on the Daily Telegraph

LETTER FROM ZAMBIA

ADEWALE MAJA-PEARCE
Cautionary tales

'Responsibility' cuts both ways, as the editor of Zambia's leading independent newspaper discovered when the government took him to court

Five years on, the pattern has become wearisomely familiar: the beleaguered Life President finally bows to the pressure for multi-party democracy, the opposition rides to power promising all the fundamental freedoms denied by the disgraced tyrant and, before one year is out the people, relegated once again to a convenient abstraction, are left wondering whether the entire exercise was worth the long wait under the hot sun.

For some, of course, the prospect of change for its own sake after 27 unbroken years of one-party rule was justification enough; but most of the people I spoke with during the elections in Zambia in late 1991 dared to hope that the former trade union leader turned presidential aspirant, Frederick Chiluba, would manage the affairs of the country with greater transparency than was practised by his predecessor, which was why they had little hesitation giving him the mandate he sought.

Alas, it was not to be. All the high-flown, pre-election rhetoric about the need to ensure the independence of the media turned out to be a ruse designed only to deceive an unsuspecting populace. At his first conference after assuming power in November 1991, for instance, President Chiluba spoke of the damage that the media could do if they said 'the wrong thing', and warned of the need for the press to be 'responsible'. This explains his subsequent refusal to privatise either of the two state-owned daily newspapers, the *Times of Zambia* and the *Zambia*

Daily Mail, or to reduce government interference in the functioning of the state-owned Zambia National Broadcasting Corporation (ZNBC), which the MMD, in its previous incarnation, had taken to court for failing to broadcast television advertisements already paid for by the party.

President Chiluba's use of the word responsible is unfortunate, not least because the definition of what constitutes responsible journalism depends largely on which side of the equation you happen to find yourself. For the politician, of course, 'responsible' generally means being favourable to the government, even to the extent of passing over in silence allegations of corruption and incompetence; for the newspaper editor, the same word usually (but not invariably) means the exact opposite, so much so that the director of one independent newspaper, Fred M'membe, recently defended his right to publish blatant untruths in the name of press freedom: 'The press does get things wrong, but so do politicians and governments. Over the last three years I have written more than 200 editorials. They might all have been wrong, but that does not bother me much. What bothers me is the prospect of not being able to write another wrong editorial...'

M'membe's paper, *The Post*, is the country's only independent publication to have been singled out by the authorities for special attention, but this is hardly surprising. With the exception of the weekly *National Mirror*, all the others — *Crime News*, *Profit*, *The Sun* and the *Weekly Express* — tend to avoid direct confrontation with the government; and the *National Mirror*, although fearless in its own way, is published by the Christian Council of Zambia. The church connection is everything. President Chiluba is himself a born-again Christian who has on more than one occasion called Zambia a Christian country despite the secular provisions of the constitution and the presence of a substantial Muslim minority. One of the first acts of the government after assuming office was to ban a Muslim radio programme (since lifted). Four licences recently awarded to private radio stations all went to Christian groups.

So, for instance, as early as March 1993, the president threatened to sue *The Post* following a series of articles the previous year accusing him of receiving a Mercedes Benz car as part of a contract worth US$18,000 with a South African company. The state prosecutor, Ali Hamir, demanded that M'membe either apologise and pay damages, or face prosecution. M'membe refused to apologise, but in the event the matter was dropped. Three months later, the paper published a report, supported by official documents, accusing a government minister of involvement in drug smuggling. The police demanded that the paper reveal its sources. M'membe declined to do so and was briefly detained. A few months later, on 16 September, a van taking 50,000 copies of the paper from Ndola, in the north, to Lusaka, the capital, was ambushed by armed men. The driver was beaten up and bundles of the paper were burnt.

Advertising The Post: *'the right to be wrong'*

In April the following year, President Chiluba charged M'membe and his assistant, Bright Mwape, with defamation following a story that quoted a former minister calling the president 'a twit'. Four months later, M'membe, together with eight of his colleagues, was charged with five counts of criminal libel against the president's press secretary, one count of criminal libel against the president, two counts of printing and possessing classified documents, and one count of publishing false stories with intent to bring fear and alarm to the public. According to the paper's lawyer, Sakwiba Sikota, the charges related to various articles which had appeared over the previous weeks, including a report that the president was involved in drug smuggling, and the publication of classified plans to scrap housing allowances for civil servants. All the cases are currently pending. In the meantime, three outstanding libel cases instituted in 1993 by Michael Sata, the then minister of labour and social services, resulted in January this year in accumulated fines of one million kwacha. (US$ 1.00 = 1,000.00 kwacha)

Ensuring that a newspaper is fined out of business is obviously the next best thing to banning it outright, a tricky proposition given the country's reliance on the goodwill of the international donor community simply to feed itself, the point being that *The Post* has hardly helped its own cause. This is nowhere better demonstrated than in the Michael Sata cases. The first was the result of an article in the 22-28 May 1992 edition accusing the minister of 'political prostitution' on the grounds that he had switched allegiance from the former ruling party to the present one when it became clear that the MMD was heading for victory in the impending elections. The article also called the minister a 'clearly dishonourable man' for apparently outrageous behaviour on television and the fact that he was the subject of an anti-corruption investigation by a commission set up for that purpose.

The second libel action concerned an article that appeared in the 31 July-6 August 1992 issue in which it was alleged that the minister had diverted 60 million kwacha earmarked for Lusaka City Council employees, and a further 1.6 billion kwacha representing salary increments for local authority employees, into a fixed deposit account for personal use on a housing project he was involved in. The article called him 'unruly' and 'greedy'. The third and final article, which appeared in the 8-14 January 1993 issue, reiterated the allegation of corrupt enrichment.

Only the most partisan observer would disagree with the ruling of the chief justice of the High Court, M M S W Ngulube, concerning the intemperate language in all three articles; and the newspaper, which has appealed against the judgment, was perhaps fortunate in a chief justice whose own commitment to the principles of free speech was spelt out unambiguously enough in his preliminary comments:

'Let me make it clear that I fully endorse the view that some recognition ought to be given to the constitutional provisions in Article 20 and I accept that impersonal criticisms of public conduct leading to injury to official reputation should generally not attract liability if there is no actual malice and even if the truth of all facts alleged is not established if the imputation complained of is competent on the remainder of the facts actually proved.'

It was for this reason that the chief justice found in favour of the plaintiff 'only in respect of the allegations that he was a 'political prostitute' and that he was 'greedy' in the first two cases, and 'the allegation of corruption' in the third. By giving hostages to fortune, in other words, *The Post* is in real danger of colluding in its own demise. ❑

LEGAL: MEDIA REGULATION

A legal column dedicated to the memory of Bernie Simons (1941-1993), radical lawyer and defender of human rights

CHRISTOPHER HIRD

Rebuffed in Britain

UK proposals to regulate media ownership irritate the biggest mogul of them all — but there's no shortage of would-be successors

'A free and diverse media are an indispensable part of the democratic process. They provide a multiplicity of voices and opinions that inform the public, influence opinion and engender political debate. They promote the culture of dissent which any healthy democracy must have. In so doing they contribute to the cultural fabric of the nation and help define our sense of identity and purpose. If one voice becomes too powerful, this process is placed in jeopardy and democracy is damaged. Special media ownership rules, which exist in all major markets, are needed therefore to provide the safeguards necessary to maintain diversity and plurality.'

The surprise about these sentiments is the author: a minister in what was once considered the most ideological of market-oriented governments in western Europe, the Conservative government of the United Kingdom. They appeared in May 1995 in the government's White Paper proposing changes in the laws governing media ownership — proposals which will almost certainly become law.

One of the people most disadvantaged by the UK government's proposals is the world's most powerful media magnate, Rupert Murdoch, and his response to them has been predictably caustic. But it would be fair to summarise the British government's proposals as a reasonably pragmatic compromise in which the aspirations of profit-seeking enterprises are moderated by the demands of more widely drawn public policy. True, the proposals don't break up the large media conglomerates but, unmoderated, such calls can be turned against public service broadcasters such as the BBC.

The key points of the British government's proposals are as follows:
• a company that controls less than 20 per cent of national newspaper circulation can control 15 per cent of the national television market;
• no company can control more than two of the commercial television licences in the UK but companies that already control 20 per cent of national newspaper circulation are restricted further to a 20 per cent share in one commercial TV company and five per cent in a second.

These rules were bad news for Rupert Murdoch whose News Corporation controls 37 per cent of Britain's national newspaper circulation. (They were also bad news for the traditionally Labour-supporting Mirror Group, which controls 26 per cent and has television ambitions.) But worse for Murdoch, the rules controlling cross-ownership between terrestrial, satellite and cable television were abolished — except for those broadcasters 'already under more than 20 per cent ownership by a newspaper with more than 20 per cent national circulation.' There was only one company this really applied to: News Corporation with its 40 per cent stake in the satellite broadcaster BSkyB.

Murdoch's response to these pro-

Rupert Murdoch: global player

posals was swift — he had a shouting match with their author, the heritage minister Stephen Dorrell and then wrote his own press release — tearing up the more measured draft of his advisers. Murdoch's press release sneered at 'this supposedly free-enterprise, pro-competition government' which had produced 'the proposals of the old vested and often unsuccessful interests' of his competitors.

It was easy to see why Murdoch was annoyed. This was not the sort of rebuff he was used to. In April he had seen off an investigation by the American Federal Communications Commission into his control of the Fox television and film business. The British policy frustrated the strategy he was developing for the rest of this decade and into the next century.

Murdoch has recently signed a deal with the USA's second largest telecommunications operator, MCI, under which MCI has invested US$2 billion in News Corporation. The deal will help Murdoch into the world of the 'information superhighway' in which traditional divisions between television and telecommunications are blurred. The evidence that there is sufficient demand to make a profitable business out of this is sparse. Murdoch himself says that he is 'sailing blind' but he cannot run the risk of not having 'access to all the different delivery systems that are emerging in the world'. In other words, as well as having a dominant position in producing the books, films, news and television programmes (the 'software') he also wants to be in control of the way these products get to the public — the printed page, the cable, the satellite and — even — the transmitter, which sends terrestrial television programmes.

This was the further significance of the MCI deal: it gave Murdoch US$2 billion dollars to invest not just in the superhighway, but also in his other media interests. And one of these is an area many thought Murdoch had turned his back on — established terrestrial European television. Within days of the MCI deal it emerged that Murdoch was negotiating with Silvio Berlusconi to buy into his three Italian stations. These account for about 40 per cent of that country's viewing audience.

One of the reasons Murdoch has developed a new appetite for television stations is closely connected to one of the other major developments in his business over the last year. Murdoch has spent a large amount of money buying up the rights to major sporting events — football in Britain, football, table tennis and badminton in China, rugby league in Australia and Britain, American football in the United States, and rugby union virtually everywhere.

Sport is the key to getting mass television audiences and, in the case of pay-television, to making it profitable. With programme assets like these in his hands, Murdoch can increase his share of the television market at a time when the deregulation tide may sweep across Europe. In May 1994 the European Council received a report which it had asked for from a group of eminent experts entitled 'Europe and the global information society'. The report — known as the Bangemann report, after its chairman — was produced by a group drawn almost exclusively from business. Its recommendations — although couched in consensus-seeking language — all drive towards a set of policy proposals which will remove many of the controls on the European media, telecommunications and information industries.

The pressures to allow a relaxation in the regulatory structures is intense and Murdoch's News Corporation — now in league with a telecommunications company — is well placed to take advantage of this.

But in the case of Britain, he was either badly advised or gambled recklessly. A few weeks before the British government published their White Paper on media ownership, the bids for Britain's fifth terrestrial channel closed. Until the last minute a consortium of which Murdoch's BSkyB was a member was expected to put in a bid of around £24 million (US$36m). At the last minute this was slashed to £2 million.

Murdoch said he thought that it was not going to be commercially successful. But it is also possible that he took a view on the forthcoming changes in British media ownership rules and reckoned that they would be relaxed — but not enough to allow him to own both Channel Five and one of the established terrestrial channels. So he sacrificed the chance of Channel Five. In fact, the new rules effectively prevented him from taking over anything — hence his rage.

In his first angry response to the White Paper Murdoch was issuing veiled threats about his commitment to Britain: 'If we have a media regulator, I'm not saying what we will do in four or five years' time.' By the weekend he had refined this to saying that he was worried that the rules would lead to UK companies being overtaken in the world media markets. 'There is much serious business to be done — for Britain,' he trumpeted.

It is not quite clear what this business is — or rather, not clear what sort of business the Murdoch approach would lead to. There is plenty of evidence that he is interested in buying up companies to grant access to airwaves for products he already owns, rather less that he is interested in making more programmes.

In a BBC interview he also petulantly threw out the challenge to nationalise him: 'I don't care if you say get out of Britain, give the world to the BBC. What sort of society do you really want? You know we got rid of that stuff when the Berlin Wall came down.'

No-one should mind if Murdoch deserts Britain — or anywhere else. It may well be true that regulation discourages companies from entering the media industry but there is no sign yet of a shortage of potential investors. Indeed, regulation itself can increase the number of people in the industry as it reduces the need for large amounts of capital. It is always possible to imagine a regulatory regime so severe that no-one would enter the business but, contrary to what Murdoch says, it is hard to see signs of such a regime in Britain at the moment. ❏

Christopher Hird produces TV documentaries. His Murdoch, the Great Escape, *was published by Warner in 1991*

INDEX INDEX

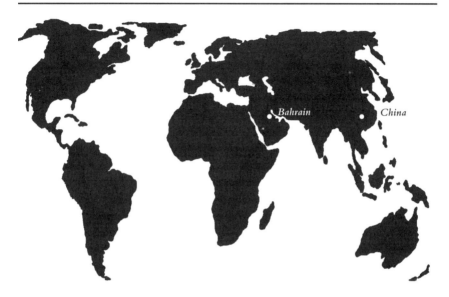

An internal affair

The Chinese government's response to criticism is simple: if it comes from inside China, the critic is locked up; if it comes from abroad, it is brushed aside as unwarranted interference in matters of domestic concern. Harry Wu presents the Chinese authorities with a double demon: as a naturalised US citizen and human rights activist, he is a critic of international renown; as an alumnus of the Chinese penal system, having spent 19 years in prisons and labour camps, he knows better than most human rights advocates the scale and brutality of China's campaign against dissident thought and action.

Faced with such a double threat, China overreacted: Wu was charged with supplying state secrets (in other words, telling the world just how bad things are in the gulag), an offence punishable by death. US public opinion, always outspoken in defence of its own citizens abroad, was outraged and, by mid-July, China realised that it had gone too far. Though the authorities maintained that the legal case against Wu was solid, it appealed to the US to be 'patient', and await the outcome of the investigation. Western diplomats took that as a sign that Wu would most likely be let out of China unharmed.

Whatever the outcome, the Wu case highlights growing tensions in Sino-US relations, following an official visit to the US by Taiwan's President Lee Teng-hui in June. It seems that China's apparent backdown over Wu was prompted by calls in the US Congress for the denial of China's most favoured nation trading status. If that is so, then President Clinton's decision a year ago to break the link between trade and human rights, looks more than ever like the wrong one. Meanwhile, in July Germany's Chancellor Kohl assured China that it has a right to its own concept of human rights, on the back of a new trade agreement between the two countries worth $3 billion.

Around 60 dissidents were arrested in the run-up to this year's Tiananmen Square anniversary, among them Chen Ziming, one of the leading protesters in 1989: he had signed a petition calling for the release of all China's political prisoners. According to Amnesty International's world report, released in July, those political prisoners number in 'the thousands'. That number is an estimate: it is impossible to verify because China does not allow human rights monitors in to the country. However many thousands they are, their cause is ill-served by a broadly compliant international community that ranks trade relations above human rights concerns.

Bahrain, too, has a government that likes to keep it all in the family. On 26 August this year it will be 20 years since the Emir suspended the Constitution and dissolved Parliament, preferring to rule by decree. In December 1994 Bahrain's discontent boiled over into demonstrations and riots against the Emir's autocratic rule, in which at least 11 people have so far died [*Index* 1/1995]. Lately, the information minister, Tariq al-Muayyad, has been trying to persuade the outside world that the extent of the disaffection has been greatly exaggerated. Bahrain, he says, is simply suffering from 'bad publicity' orchestrated by hostile foreign media bent on undermining stability in the Gulf.

In an attempt to stem the flow of bad publicity, the Information Ministry now requires any citizen who wants to send news of their country to the press abroad to obtain an 'accredited licence' from the Directorate of Public Relations and Media. ❑

Adam Newey

A censorship chronicle incorporating information from the American Association for the Advancement of Science Human Rights Action Network (AAASHRAN), Amnesty International (AI), Article 19 (A19), the BBC Monitoring Service Summary of World Broadcasts (SWB), Centro de Periodistas para la Libertad de Expresión (CEPEX), the Committee to Protect Journalists (CPJ), the Canadian Committee to Protect Journalists (CCPJ), Human Rights Watch (HRW), the Inter-American Press Association (IAPA), the International Federation of Journalists (IFJ/FIP), the International Federation of Newspaper Publishers (FIEJ), the Media Institute of Southern Africa (MISA), International PEN (PEN), Open Media Research Institute Daily Digest (OMRI), Reporters Sans Frontières (RSF) and other sources

ALBANIA

Four men were arrested in Gjirocastra in May for founding a Communist party. Communist parties have been banned since 1992. (OMRI)

The mayor of Tirana banned the sale of newspapers on the street from 1 June, restricting sale to 20 state-owned outlets. Following the ban, police have reportedly been harassing street news vendors. (*Independent*, International Press Institute)

On 1 June the gay association Shoqata Gay Albania was legally registered with the Justice Ministry, in accordance with the new Penal Code, which legalises homosexual relations between consenting adults. (Reuter)

Filip Cakuli of *Hosteni 2000* was arrested and interrogated for 12 hours by secret police on 20 June, during production of an issue of the paper which was to feature a front-cover caricature of President Berisha with two naked women. (IFJ)

Recent publication: *Failure to End Police Ill-Treatment and Deaths in Custody* (AI, June 1995, 28pp)

ALGERIA

The murder of journalists continues: Azzedine Saidj, editor-in-chief of the now-closed *El Ouma*, was found murdered in his car on 15 May; Malika Sabour of *Echourouk al-Arabi* was killed in her home on 21 May by attackers who posed as policemen to gain entry to her home; Bakhti Benaouda, a professor at Oran University who also wrote for the government daily *El Djoumhouria* and the literary journal *Al-Karmel*, was shot dead in Oran on 22 May; Mourad Hmaizi of the state broadcaster ENTV, was shot dead in Oued Smar on 27 May; and Ahmed Taakoucht, alias Hakim, a journalist with Constantine local radio station Cirta, had his throat cut on 18 June. (RSF, Reuter)

Several publications have been suspended either because of newsprint shortage or by order of the communications minister. The 30 May edition of the government-run paper *Horizons* was banned for suggesting that the paper shortage was a deliberate policy to undermine the press. On 7 June the minister suspended three papers, *El Ouma* (Index 6/1994) for 15 days, and the weeklies *La Nation* (Index 2/1995) and *El-Houriyya* for one month each, for publishing an appeal co-signed by the Islamic Salvation Front (FIS) and eight other political parties, calling for a 'people's assembly'. On 19 June the weeklies *El Hadith* and *El-Maw'id* were suspended for six months for unknown reasons. (RSF, SWB)

ARMENIA

Most of Armenia's religious groups suffered attacks in what appeared to be a systematic campaign by government officials in April. Groups of Jehovah's Witnesses, Hare Krishnas, Pentecostal and Charismatic Christians, Seventh Day Adventists and Bahais saw raids on their premises, assaults on their members, and destruction of property. Government paramilitaries warned during some of the raids that any one preaching against army conscription would not be tolerated. Some groups later received official apologies for the attacks. (News Network International)

The Russian-language daily *Golos Armenii* stopped production on 11 May following refusal by the state printing house, Periodika, to continue producing it. Following public

INDEX INDEX

pressure, President Ter-Pretosian intervened directly to enable production to resume later in the month. Many other opposition papers linked to the banned Dachnaksoutioun party, however, remain closed (*Index* 2/1995). (RSF)

Around 10 people were injured during a demonstration held on 21 June in Yerevan. They were protesting the authorities' refusal to grant permits for several political parties to field candidates in the 5 July parliamentary elections. (OMRI)

BAHRAIN

Pro-democracy activist Sheikh Abd al-Amir Mansur al-Jamri (*Index* 3/1995), remains in detention. It is believed that he is being held in connection with a petition he drafted in June 1994 calling for the re-establishment of Parliament and the restoration of the Constitution. (PEN)

Over 40 people who took part in ongoing pro-democracy demonstrations (*Index* 1/1995, 3/1995) were sentenced to prison terms ranging from one year to life after secret trials, without legal representation, in late June. One man, Issa Qambar, was sentenced to death for his alleged part in the killing of a security officer. At least 11 civilians have so far been killed in the protests. A further 33 detainees are due to be tried in the coming weeks. (Bahrain Human Rights Organisation, Bahrain Freedom Movement)

BELARUS

Since the referendum of 14 May, which gave equal status to Russian as the state language, there have been various moves to downgrade the status of Belarusian. The Ministry of Culture has cancelled its promised subsidies for over 70 books which had previously been scheduled to form part of an official programme to raise the status of the language. The axed titles include a complete edition of the works of the national poet, Janka Kupala (1882-1942), which would have included several works banned by the Soviet censors, reprints of major works by emigre writers and classics from the Belarusian revival of the early twentieth century. (*Times Higher Educational Supplement*)

An edition of the current affairs programme *Corridors* was banned after a preliminary viewing on 10 May. The programme dealt with the events of 11-12 April, when democratic deputies staging a protest fast were forcibly removed from Parliament (*Index* 3/1995). (SWB)

The authorities have resumed jamming of the US-funded station Radio Liberty. This is the first time the station has been jammed since the Soviet era. (*Obshchaya Gazeta*, Jamestown *Monitor*)

Catholic religious programmes in Belarusian have been dropped from TV, and it is forbiddent to broadcast the patriotic hymn 'O God Almighty, O Lord of Creation'. Belarusian folk songs are to be broadcast in Russian translation, and most if not all Belarusian pop music is not to be carried at all. A traditional midsummer's eve festival in Minsk was cancelled by the city council minutes before it was due to start. As the crowd dispersed, the lead singer of 'New Heaven' pop group sang them off with the latest subversive hit, 'Go home, Mr President'. (*Eastern Europe Newsletter*)

BELGIUM

Police searched the offices of the dailies *Le Soir* and *De Morgen*, the magazine *Le Soir Illustré*, and the broadcast network RTBF on 23 June. The homes of several journalists were also searched. The police were investigating possible illegal leaks from magistrates to the media about the ongoing confidential probe into a scandal over defence contracts. (RSF)

BOSNIA-HERCEGOVINA

Journalist Namik Berberovic (*Index* 3/1995) reports that he met jailed Serbian poet Vladimir Srebov while in a Bosnian Serb prison, and that Srebov is in very poor health. Srebov is being held on charges of 'high treason and war crimes' but the length of his sentence is unclear. (PEN)

Italian journalist Matteo Toson of *Avvenimenti* and *Informazione*, reported missing in April, was arrested by Bosnian police on 16 May and released on 5 June in Sarajevo. He had gone to

Sarajevo from Belgrade to investigate weapons trafficking. (RSF)

On 28 June a Bosnian Serb rocket attack on the television building in Sarajevo killed a policemen and injured dozens of people, including journalists working for Worldwide Television News and Associated Press TV. WTN, APTV and European Broadcasting Union offices in the building were completely destroyed. Observers believe the attack was a deliberate attempt to kill reporters. (IFJ, *Independent, Guardian*)

BRAZIL

The governor of the state of Amazonas has issued an order denying journalists from the Manaus daily *A Critica* access to information on the public sector, it was reported in late May. The order was apparently made in response to critical remarks made in *A Critica* by a member of the state legislature on the running of state enterprises. (IAPA)

A draft bill on taxing newsprint was approved by the Constitution and Justice Committee of the lower house of the legislature in early June. Press advocates fear a new tax might be used to undermine newspapers' independence. (IAPA)

BULGARIA

In May Parliament cancelled a US$646,000 contribution to the Open Society Fund set up by financier George Soros. Parliamentary chairman Blagovest Sendor reportedly accused Soros of interfering in domestic affairs, after he expressed his concern about a number of xenophobic publications in Bulgaria. The fund finances the American University in Blagoevgrad, scholarships, scientific projects and exchanges. (OMRI)

On 23 June Parliament voted to replace television chief Hacho Boyadzhiev and radio chief Ivan Obretenov with Ivan Granitski and Veheslav Tunev, formerly of the daily *24 Hours*. The ruling Socialist Party, which pushed the decisions through Parliament, said that national television 'frequently erodes national values and substitutes them for cheap foreign subcultural products'. Opposition politicians accuse the government of undermining the political independence of the broadcast media. (Reuter, SWB)

BURMA

On 8 June, diplomatic sources reported that Kyi Maung, a senior National League for Democracy member, had been arrested after a meeting with the British ambassador. The dissident, who had been freed in March after five years in prison, was detained along with four or five others. Kyi Maung became NLD leader after Aung San Suu Kyi and other leaders were arrested in 1989. (*Times*)

On 19 June the International Committee of the Red Cross (ICRC) announced it was closing its office in Burma because it cannot get acceptable access to political prisoners. The ICRC said that after 10 months' consideration, the ruling State Law and Order Restoration Council had refused the organisation's standard requirements: to have private meetings with prisoners, to be able to visit all prisons, and to be assured of repeat visits. (*Guardian*)

Aung San Suu Kyi (*Index* 4&5/1994) was unconditionally released from house arrest on 10 July. However, at least 10 more writers and journalists — Myo Myint Nyein, Sein Hlaing, Nay Min, Nyi Pu Lay, Ohn Kyaing, Win Tin, San San Nwe, Ma Myat Mo Mo Tun, U Sein Hla Oo and Khin Zaw Win — remain in prison, serving sentences of up to 20 years. (PEN)

Recent publications: *No Place to Hide* (AI, June 1995, 37pp); *Aung San Suu Kyi* (AI, June 1995, 4pp)

BURUNDI

Pamphile Sambizi, the director of the French section of the state radio station, was stabbed to death on 7 June in Bujumbura. Sambizi was part of the moderate Hutu movement at the station. The motive for his murder is unknown. (RSF)

Nine students, most of them Hutus, were killed on 12 June when Tutsi students fired machine-guns and threw hand grenades into dormitories on the Mutanga campus in Bujumbura, in retaliation for an earlier Hutu attack on

INDEX INDEX

Tutsi schoolchildren in which four died. On 21 June a Hutu professor was also killed in his office at Bujumbura University. No progress has yet been made with an official inquiry into the killings. (Reuter)

In June Reporters Sans Frontières submitted a complaint against the newspapers *L'Etoile*, *La Nation*, *Le Carrefour des Idées*, *Le Temoin* and *L'Eclaireur* to the National Communication Council, and filed complaints against *L'Etoile*, *La Nation* and *Le Carrefour des Idées* with the attorney-general's office in Bujumbura for incitement to murder. RSF have also called on the United Nations to take action against extremist publications. The prime minister called for UN help on 8 July in closing down the pirate radio station Rutomorangingo, which is said to be inciting ethnic hatred. (RSF, Reuter, SWB)

Recent publications: *The Venom of Hate* (RSF, June 1995, 96pp); *Struggle for Survival* (AI, June 1995, 23pp)

CAMBODIA

The former finance minister, Sam Rainsy, was expelled from the National Assembly on 22 June. Rainsy was stripped of the finance portfolio in October 1994 and expelled from the ruling FUNCINPEC party in May 1995. He has been a fierce critic of government corruption at all levels and recently announced that he was setting up a new opposition party.

Rainsy described the expulsion as illegal and said he continued to consider himself a member of the Assembly. (*Guardian*, Reuter)

By 10 July the National Assembly had reviewed 12 of the 22 articles in the controversial draft Press Law (*Index* 1/1995). The most significant provisions agreed so far are those requiring would-be editors or publishers to prove that they have no criminal record; an absolute prohibition on reproducing 'information which affects national security and political stability', and a broadly worded statement on incitement. Some Assembly members criticised the vague wording of the security and stability provision, which also grants the Information Ministry powers to shut down offending publications for 30 days and to levy fines against individual journalists and publishers, regardless of further possible punishments under the penal code for the same offence. (International Human Rights Law Group)

CAMEROON

Twelve thousand copies of *Le Messager* (*Index* 2/1995) were seized as they left the presses in Douala on 15 May, the third day running that an issue was confiscated in this way. The paper's editor, Pius Njawe, says the seizures are intended to bankrupt it. (RSF, SWB)

On 6 June police raided the home of Ndzana Seme, editor-in-chief of the daily *Le Nouvel Indépendant*. His house is also the paper's office. Two journalists and nine office workers were beaten by police, who arrested Seme for insulting the head of state and 'incitement to rebellion'. The arrest is believed to be connected to articles alleging corruption in government and in the police force. (Reuter, RSF)

CHAD

Soldiers entered the offices of the weekly paper *N'Djamena Hebdo* on 1 June and arrested the director, Dieudonne Djonabaye, and his assistant, Yaldet Begoto Oulatar. The soldiers destroyed most of the office equipment and beat other members of staff. Oulatar and Djonabaye were released later that night after having been beaten in detention. The paper's editor had previously been summoned before the ministers of information and defence after an article on 4 May alleged that the Chadian army employed Sudanese mercenaries. At a meeting on 6 June, President Deby told a group of independent newspaper directors that the raid had been 'a mistake'. (PEN, Reuter, SWB)

Recent publication: *Empty Promises: Human Rights Violations Continue with Impunity* (AI, 27 April 1995, 27pp)

CHINA

In May and early June eight petitions signed by more than 100 scientists, intellectuals, and human rights activists were presented to the authorities and the Communist Party leadership, calling for tolerance and the release of political prisoners. Shortly after the first two petitions appeared on 15 and 19 May, leading signatories were detained and others harassed by government officials. Among the detainees were Wang Xizhe, Liu Xiaobo, Huang Xiang, Zhang Ling, Wang Dan (*Index* 1&2/1995), Liu Nianchun, Jiang Qisheng, Gou Qinghui and Fu Guoyong. Huang and Liu Xiaobo are thought to be still in detention. (*Times*, CPJ, AI, AAASHRAN)

Nick Rufford, Hong Kong correspondent for the London *Sunday Times*, was arrested in his Beijing hotel room on 24 May, and held incommunicado for over 13 hours. He was accused of carrying a forged passport and visa and ordered to reveal his contacts in China. During his interrogation he was allegedly threatened with imprisonment and beaten. He was subsequently expelled to Hong Kong and his film was confiscated. (RSF, *Sunday Times*)

The Foreign Ministry criticised the award of FIEJ's Golden Pen of Freedom to imprisoned journalist Gao Yu (*Index* 10/1993, 6/1994) on 2 June, saying that it 'not only constitutes wanton interference in China's internal affairs, but blasphemes the internationally recognised principles of press freedom'. (SWB)

In the days leading up to the sixth anniversary of the Tiananmen protests on 4 June police ordered inhabitants of Beijing's 'artists' village' to move away, and set up a checkpoint on the approach to the village. Bars around the universities were closed and gatherings organised by foreigners in public places banned for five days either side of the anniversary. (*Times*, *Independent*)

Harry Wu, a naturalised US citizen and human rights activist, was detained as he crossed the border from Kazakhstan into China on 19 June. Chinese authorities originally said Wu had been detained for illegally entering restricted areas last year, while he was working with a BBC television crew, secretly filming prison labour camps. On 8 July Wu was charged with 'stealing state secrets', an offence that carries the death penalty. (AAASHRAN, *Independent*, *Observer*)

The Central Committee's propaganda department held a seminar for editors from 21 to 30 June, on how to fulfil the task of 'guiding the people with correct opinions'. (SWB)

On 25 June Chen Ziming (*Index* 3/1994), a leader of the 1989 pro-democracy protests, was arrested and returned to prison in Beijing to serve the remainder of his 13-year sentence. Originally released on medical parole, Chen's arrest is thought to be linked to his endorsement of one of the May petitions and his daylong fast marking the Tiananmen anniversary. The authorities claim that his parole has expired and his cancer has been cured. Public Security Bureau officers searched his apartment and confiscated a computer, fax machine, books, letters and other personal material. (AAASHRAN, PEN)

Recent publications: *Keeping the Lid on Demands for Change* (HRW/Asia, June 1995, 13pp); *Leaking Official Secrets: The Case of Gao Yu* (Human Rights in China and HRW/Asia, June 1995, 32pp); *Women Imprisoned and Abused for Dissent* (AI, June 1995, 27pp); *Six Years After Tiananmen: Increased Political Repression and Human Rights Violations* (AI, June 1995, 40pp)

COLOMBIA

The Senate passed an anti-corruption law on 30 May, which contains provisions to prevent journalists from reporting on investigations or legal action taken against public officials. The law would also severely restrict journalists' access to public documents and information on public officials under investigation for corruption. (CPJ)

Henry de Jesús Rendón, a leading member of the civic movement United for Progress, has disappeared following his abduction by two men in Puerto Nare on 31 May. Shortly before his disappearance, he was publicly threatened by a paramilitary group. (AI)

Luis Gabriel Caldas, a conscientious objector, was arrested on 10 June and sentenced to seven months' imprisonment by a military court for 'desertion' after he refused to undertake military service. Although conscientious objectors have the right to perform an alternative, civilian service, Caldas has been ordered to complete his military service on the expiration of his prison term, or face renewed imprisonment. (AI)

The alleged leaders of the Calí drug cartel won a court injunction on 7 July banning an advertisement carried by the television station Inravision and paid for by the government, offering a reward for their capture. (SWB)

CONGO

It was reported in late June that the publishing managers of the periodicals *La Rue Meurt*, *Le Guardien* and *Le Forum* are to be prosecuted for publishing a document purporting to be a letter from the finance minister to the head of state, Pascal Lissouba, asking him to extend his presidential mandate, which expires in 1997. Two of the three — Jean-Paul Bassouri and Gil Andal Leguette — have refused to appear before the prosecutor for fear of being arrested. The third, Massengo Tiesse of *Le Forum*, is currently in France. (SWB)

Dominique Marseille Asie, director and editor-in-chief of the weekly *Le Choc*, was arrested in Brazzaville on 22 June. Although no reason has been given for the arrest, it is thought to be in connection with a satirical article entitled 'The Union of Warlocks' in the previous week's edition of the paper. (RSF)

Mitte Miete Likidi, editor-in-chief of the state radio station, was dismissed on 5 July for releasing embargoed information about planned salary cuts for public employees. The information had already been released by several international media. (RSF)

COSTA RICA

On 9 May the Supreme Court declared that the licensing of journalists, which has been obligatory since 1969, is unconstitutional. The ruling, which is retroactive, was made in response to an appeal brought in 1990 by broadcaster Roger Ajun, who was found guilty of illegally practising journalism, and it opens the way for several other journalists to resume their profession. (IAPA)

COTE D'IVOIRE

On 9 June two journalists with the opposition weekly *La Patrie* lost their appeal against a one-year prison sentence and a fine of 2 million francs for insulting the president (*Index* 3/1995). The court of appeal also banned *La Patrie* for three months. (SWB)

On 14 June Abou Drahamane Sangare, publishing manager of the *La Voie* and *Nouvel Horizon* group of newspapers and deputy leader of the opposition Ivorian Popular Front (FPI), was summoned to the offices of the security minister, General Kone, where he was allegedly beaten. Sangare had to spend the night in hospital. The beating was apparently provoked by an article in the satirical magazine *Bol Kotch*, referring to Kone's response to student unrest. (Reuter)

CROATIA

Copies of the independent satirical weekly *Feral Tribune* were publicly burned in Split town centre on 26 and 27 June. Television crews were present but no police attended either incident. *Feral Tribune* editors suspect that members of the ruling party may be behind the action, claiming that warnings of an 'operation' were received in advance. (OMRI, *Feral Tribune*)

Recent publication: *The Croatian Army Offensive in Western Slavonia and its Aftermath* (HRW/Helsinki, July 1995, 17pp)

CUBA

Six political prisoners — Yndamiro Restano Díaz (*Index* 5/1992, 8/1992), Sebastián Arcos Bergnes (*Index* 6/1990, 2/1993), Agustín Figueredo, Pedro Castillo Ferrera, Salvia Ricardo and Luis González Ogra — were released unconditionally before the expiration of their sentences on 1 June. (Reuter)

Three members of the unofficial Association of Independent Cuban Journalists (APIC) — Orestes Sondevila, Luis López Prendes and

Lázaro Lazo — were detained by State Security officers on 8 July and interrogated about an APIC news report on a public display of criticism of the government by a retired military officer. The report was carried by the US station Radio Martí. The three men were released within two days, and were told that the government will tolerate APIC's work, but that certain stories cannot be covered. On 10 July State Security police searched the home of APIC president Néstor Baguer and confiscated his fax machine and documents. (CPJ, APIC)

Rafael Solano, Juan Lezy Isquierdo and José Rivero García of the independent agency Havana Press were arrested on 12 July. Solano has been indicted for spreading enemy propaganda in 'damaging articles sent to subversive publications'. (AI)

EGYPT

The authorities banned a human rights workshop on video technology due to be held by the American Lawyers Committee and the Egyptian Organisation for Human Rights in May. Six video cameras to be used in the workshop were confiscated at Cairo airport from Lawyers Committee representative Neil Hicks as he arrived in the country. (Reuter)

On 27 May Parliament overwhelmingly approved a bill expanding the 1937 libel law to punish journalists who spread 'libel, misinformation and "opposing" information' with heavy fines and jail terms of at least five years. Penalties can be imposed on journalists who defame public officials or institutions, or who are deemed to have harmed the country's economy. The law also allows police to detain journalists while they are under investigation. President Mubarak commented: 'I am with the freedom of the press and not the freedom to offend. The amended law will not affect those who write honourably and with trust.' (*Guardian*, RSF)

On 14 June a court overturned a ruling made in January 1994 and ordered that Nasr Abu-Zeid (*Index* 7/1993, 1&2/1994), a Cairo University professor, should be forcibly separated from his wife, Ebtihal Younis, on the grounds that he is an apostate and therefore should not be married to a Muslim woman. A Muslim militant group, Jihad, has threatened to kill Abu-Zeid. (*Independent*, Reuter)

Badea Sobhy, a cinema owner, was sentenced to three months' hard labour on 1 July for displaying a film poster featuring an actress in a low-cut dress, after a case was brought against him by Muslim activists. The poster was advertising *Layali Lan Taoud* (Unrepeatable Nights). (Reuter)

The Mufti of Egypt, Sheikh Muhammed Sayyid Tantawi, said in an interview on 2 July that Islam supports 'artistic and cultural creativity that enhances moral values, principles and chastity', but that if such creativity 'departs from this context, it is not regarded as genuine creativity'. He was speaking about Salman Rushdie's book *The Satanic Verses* which, he said, was full of 'lies and fallacies that have nothing to do with religion'. (SWB)

Recent publication: *Freedom of Opinion and Belief: Restrictions and Dilemmas* (Egyptian Organisation for Human Rights, 1995, 189pp)

EQUATORIAL GUINEA

Recent publication: *A Dismal Record of Broken Promises* (AI, July 1995, 19pp)

ETHIOPIA

The ruling Ethiopian People's Revolutionary Democratic Front (EPRDF) swept to victory in the May elections, which were boycotted by many of the opposition parties (*Index* 3/1995). Voting in the Afar, Somali and Hareri regions was delayed until 18 June because of 'logistical problems'. Western diplomats in Addis Ababa and the Organisation of African Unity have declared the elections free and fair. EPRDF leader, Meles Zenawi, will be elected prime minister, with strong executive powers, when the new Parliament meets in September. (Reuter)

Twedros Kebede, editor of the paper *Zog*, was sentenced to one year in prison on 6 July for 'printing groundless allegations and rumours' about the activities of armed opposition groups. (SWB)

Recent publication: *Accountability Past and Present* (AI, April 1995, 58pp)

EUROPEAN UNION

A report submitted to the EU summit in Cannes in June by the Consultative Commission on Racism and Xenophobia proposed legal sanctions against any media that breach ethical guidelines. Media advocates argue that regulation of journalistic ethics should be left to journalists themselves. (IFJ)

Recent publication: *Protection of Journalists' Sources: Comparative Law and Jurisprudence (Written Comments Submitted to the European Court of Human Rights in the Case of William Goodwin v. the United Kingdom* (A19/Interights, April 1995, 16pp)

FRANCE

Unions called a strike among journalists at the television station France 3 on 17 May to protest the dismissal of Philippe Descamps. Descamps was sacked after exposing financial scandals in the RPR administration in Grenoble, in which the head of France 3, Yves Le Boucher d'Herouville, was implicated. (*Guardian*)

On 21 June a representative of the government broadcasting authority (CSA), backed by police, entered the community station Radio Agora in Grasse and confiscated transmission equipment. The station is said to be broadcasting on a frequency that could have interfered with security communications during the EU meeting in Cannes. Radio Agora has been broadcasting for 10 years on the same frequency without trouble, and with regular contact with the CSA. The station reopened in July. (AMARC, CCPJ)

GEORGIA

Fr Basil of the Lomisa Church in Tbilisi was reported on 22 June to have been abducted. He had recently been suspended by the head of the Georgian Orthodox Church for speaking out against the death sentences imposed on two associates of former President Gamsakhurdia. (Georgian Human Rights Association, SWB)

GREECE

Greek authorities were accused in May of discriminating against foreign journalists by withholding access to official information, and requiring them to obtain a second accreditation before being able to attend press briefings. Some foreign journalists report receiving anonymous telephone calls, and one has received death threats. On 20 June a home-made bomb exploded in the entrance to the Foreign Press Association building in Athens. (RSF, SWB)

Journalist Vassilis Rafailidis was sentenced to four months in prison in June for insulting the mayor of Protosani, Constantin Raias. Rafailidis wrote an editorial in *Ethnos* in December 1994, accusing Raias of intolerance towards Jehovah's Witnesses. Rafailidis is currently free, pending appeal. (RSF)

GUATEMALA

On 9 April María de León Santiago, a local leader of the National Committee of Widows in Guatemala (CONAVIGUA), was attacked in her home in Vitzal, Nebaj. In March she had led a demonstration of Mayan people to Guatemala City. (AI)

Guatemala's Catholic bishops launched an alternative Truth Commission under the slogan 'Recovering the Historic Memory' on 24 April. Archbishop Prospero Penados del Barrio said that the Commission would seek to break the 'silence imposed by fear'. The project is in response to popular frustration with the official Truth Commission, set up by the UN, which is scheduled to spend only six months investigating 35 years of violence. (*Latinamerica Press*)

Lawyer Julio Eduardo Atrango Escobar, Angel Urízar, a soldier, and Jennifer Harbury have received death threats in connection with their efforts to establish the fate of Harbury's husband, Efraín Bámaca (*Index* 3/1995). On 15 June pressure from the army halted exhumations within the San Marcos military base, where Bámaca is believed to be buried. (AI, Reuter)

HAITI

Captain Lawrence Rockwood, a counter-intelli-

EUROPEAN UNION - INDIA

gence officer with the 10th Mountain Division, has been dismissed from the US army after a court martial. On 30 September 1994, while serving in Haiti, Captain Rockwood inspected a prison on his own initiative after failing to get official permission to do so. Rockwood argued that he was following the orders of his commander-in-chief, President Clinton, who had said that one aim of the US intervention was to investigate human rights abuses. (*Guardian*)

HONDURAS

On 28 June the national human rights commissioner, Leo Valladares, said that he would ask the US embassy to declassify documents relating to the disappearance of 184 Honduran civic leaders during the 1980s. The Honduran Armed Forces have burned all their files on the disappearances. (SWB)

Recent publication: *The Beginning of the End of Impunity?* (AI, June 1995, 16pp)

HONG KONG

Political cartoonist Larry Feign was dismissed from the *South China Morning Post* on 20 May. The dismissal was one of many staff cuts and editor-in-chief David Armstrong insists that it was an economic decision. Feign's strip, 'Lily Wong', was notoriously critical of China and his colleagues believe that one of his last published cartoons, which focused on organ transplants from executed criminals, may have displeased the paper's owner, Robert Kuok. (*Times, Independent*)

On 21 June reporters from *Ping Kuo Jih Pao* (Apple Daily), a new Chinese-language paper, were barred from covering a meeting in Beijing of the Preliminary Working Committee, convened to discuss the 1997 transfer of the colony. The paper is owned by Jimmy Lai, a well-known critic of the Chinese government. (Reuter)

Recent publication: *Broken Promises: Freedom of Expression in Hong Kong* (A19 and Hong Kong Journalists' Association, June 1995, 44pp)

HUNGARY

On 29 May employees of Hungarian television announced a one-day strike to protest the government's plan to privatise one of the two national channels. Four opposition parties issued a statement on 1 June, expressing their 'shock' at the government's draft media bill, which was subsequently passed for preliminary debate in Parliament on 21 June. (OMRI, SWB)

INDIA

Homosexual rights activist Ashok Row-Kavi provoked calls for the banning of Rupert Murdoch's STAR TV after he called Mahatma Gandhi a 'bastard' during the talk show *Nikki Tonight* on 4 May. The show has been suspended. Parliament accused STAR of 'cultural terrorism', and on 4 July a bailable warrant was issued against Murdoch and four others in

INDEX INDEX

connection with 'a prima facie case of insult and defamation'. (Reuter, SWB)

The government decided to let the notorious Terrorist and Disruptive Activities Act (TADA) lapse on 23 May. During its 10 years on the statute book, TADA was used to keep thousands of innocent people in prison. The government's decision follows years of campaigning by human rights groups and Muslim organisations, who argued they were unfairly targeted by the act. (Reuter)

Members of the Kashmir press corps and visiting correspondents walked out of a press conference called by election commissioner T N Shesan in Srinagar on 27 May after he refused to address a British Broadcasting Corporation (BBC) reporter. Apparently Shesan had taken offence at another BBC correspondent after a previous interview. Earlier in May, in Assam state, Shesan insisted that a reporter leave a press conference because he asked 'funny questions'. (Reuter)

The government revoked its ban on the ultra-nationalist Vishwa Hindu Parishad party (VHP) on 20 June. The ban had been in force since the 1992 destruction of the Babri mosque in Ayodhya. The VHP is influential among one section of the Bharatiya Janata Party (BHP), the main opposition party. (Reuter)

State-run Doordarshan television signed an agreement with Turner International, which owns Cable News Network (CNN), on 2 July allowing CNN to broadcast to India. In return Doordarshan will get some broadcasting time on CNN, but opposition groups accuse the government of selling out India's national interests. The government is also said to be trying to counter the influence of the BBC in the region, in particular the coverage it has given to Kashmiri separatists. (Reuter)

Abdul Rashid Shah, editor of *Nedia-e-Mashrig*, and Bashir Manzar, associate editor of *Greater Kashmir*, were kidnapped by a militant group on 6 July. The kidnappers said they would release the pair on 9 July, but have not as yet done so. (SWB)

Recent publication: *Rape for Profit: Trafficking of Nepali Girls and Women to India's Brothels* (HRW/Asia, July 1995, 90pp)

INDONESIA

Academic and human rights activist George Aditjondro (*Index* 6/1994, 3/1995) said on 5 June that he is to apply for permanent residence in Australia, where he is on a visiting fellowship. (SWB)

The trial of Alliance of Independent Journalists journalists Ahmad Taufik and Eko Maryadi (*Index* 3/1995) started in Jakarta on 16 June. They are charged with 'sowing hatred against the government', insulting President Suharto and violating the Press Act. In a separate trial, AJI assistant Danang Kukuh is charged with 'expressing hatred against the state and president'. Despite a ban on the AJI paper *Independens* by the attorney-general's office, the AJI has vowed to continue producing it. A new version of the paper, *Suara Independens* (Voice of Independence), was launched in June by AJI members in Amsterdam. (*Straits Times*)

The information minister warned on 22 June that publication of a dummy issue of the banned magazine *Tempo* would require a licence and that the authorities would take action if journalists went ahead without one. The dummy edition, planned to mark the first anniversary of the magazine's banning on 21 June, was to have a limited circulation among parliamentarians, journalists and private companies. (Reuter)

On 28 June the information minister called for an immediate halt to the sale of imported uncensored laser discs. The continuing availability of the discs was, he said, 'spreading poison in our society'. Although his comments were primarily aimed at films with high levels of sex and violence, the authorities are also concerned at the effect of imports on the indigenous film industry. (*Jakarta Post*)

Recent publication: *Workers' Rights Still Challenged* (AI, June 1995, 15pp)

IRAN

A group of 86 political activists voiced criticisms of the government in an open statement in April. They charge the government with being ineffective, corrupt, and with having ruined the economy. They also condemn the current US sanctions against Iran for punishing ordinary citizens. (*About Iran*)

The *Tehran Times* reported on 7 June that European governments should not have allowed the Rushdie affair to mar relations with Iran. It said western commentators were wrong to describe the *fatwa* as a 'death sentence' because 'it is a religious decree which can be applied to all domains of a man's life.' (SWB)

IRAQ

RSF reports that, as of June 1995, nine journalists are being held in prison in Iraq. However, neither their names nor their year of arrest has so far been established. (RSF)

IRELAND

It was reported on 12 May that television viewers in Ireland will be able to watch the satellite station Playboy TV, notwithstanding a permanent ban on the magazine. The station is expected to begin transmission to Ireland early next year. (*Irish Times*)

On 14 May the Irish College of General Practioners approved an information pack for family doctors, allowing them to tell women for the first time where and at what cost an abortion can be obtained in Britain. Doctors opposed to abortion are not, however, under any obligation to provide the information to patients. (*Irish Times*)

ISRAEL

Mordechai Vanunu (*Index* 6/1994/, 3/1995), jailed in 1986 for exposing Israel's nuclear programme, has appealed for better prison conditions after nearly nine years in solitary confinement in Ashkelon jail, south of Tel Aviv. The military censor permitted a forum entitled 'Nuclear Weaponry, News Media and Public Opinion' to take place at Haifa University on 16 May, a possible indication of Israel's willingness to allow debate on its nuclear policy. (*Times*, *Sunday Times*, Campaign to Free Vanunu)

Photographer Abbas Momani was beaten by Israeli soldiers on 23 June while covering a demonstration at Al-Jalazon refugee camp. He was subsequently arrested while covering disturbances in Ramallah and sentenced by a military court to 15 days in prison on 6 July. On 24 June three journalists, Khaled Az-Zighari (*Index* 6/1994), a photographer for Reuter, Awad Awad of photo agency Zoom 77, and Atta Aweissat (*Index* 1&2/1994) were assaulted by police while covering a demonstration in East Jerusalem. (RSF)

Thousands of Christians demonstrated in Haifa, Jaffa, Nazareth and Sahfa Amr against the broadcast on 7 May of Martin Scorsese's 1988 film *The Last Temptation of Christ* by the Haifa-based cable company Second Showing. The Israeli High Court rejected a petition to ban the film. (*Jerusalem Times*)

Recent publication: *A Policy of Discrimination: Land Expropriation, Planning and Building in East Jerusalem* (B'Tselem, May 1995, 91pp)

KENYA

On 27 June attorney-general Amos Wako announced a new bill to ban members of existing parties from forming or helping to form other parties. The measure would directly affect human rights lawyers and opposition parliamentarians, Paul Muite and Kiraitu Murungi, who are involved with the formation of the Sarafina party, launched by conservationist Richard Leakey on 7 May, and is seen as a potential threat to the ruling KANU party. (Reuter)

Police arrested Mirugi Kariuki and Paul Muite, the laywers leading the defence of Koigi wa Wamwere (*Index* 2/1995), along with a Zambian representative of the International Commission of Jurists and two Norwegian journalists on 22 May at Bahati police station, the station where wa Wamwere is accused of having carried out an armed robbery. The five were accused of assaulting a police officer, but released the following day. (AI, SWB)

LEBANON

On 28 June Beirut's Publications Court issued its first custodial sentences in 23 years, sentencing Hassan Sabra

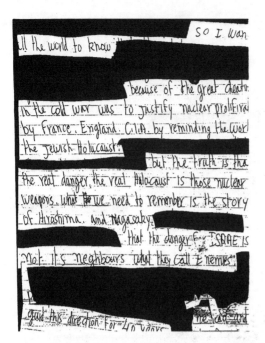

Excerpts from a heavily censored letter sent by Mordechai Vanunu to Fredrik Heffermehl, Vice-President of the International Peace Bureau in Oslo, dated 19 February and received on 27 March 1995

and Ghazi al-Maqhur (*Index* 7/1992), publisher and managing editor respectively of *Al-Shira* magazine, to one month each in jail for defaming President Elias Hrawi in a 1991 article entitled 'Reform or resign'. Youssef al-Howeyyek, director of the Beirut daily *al-Diyar*, was sentenced to three months' jail and fined 50 million Lebanese pounds (US$31,000) for slandering an MP. The journalists are appealing against the sentences. (CPJ, Reuter)

MACAO

The editor-in-chief of *Gazeta Macaense*, Paulo Reis (*Index* 3/1995), was found guilty of 'abusing press freedom' in late June. He received a three-month prison sentence, which was suspended for two years, and was ordered to pay US$5,000 compensation to the head of the Supreme Court, Farinhas Ribeiras, and to publish the full text of his sentence in his newspaper. (*Gazeta Macaense*)

The entire Macao consignment of the recently launched Hong Kong paper *Ping Kuo Jih Pao* (Apple Daily) was seized and thrown into the harbour by a group of men on 28 June. The paper is owned by the controversial Hong Kong boutique chain proprietor, Jimmy Lai (*Index* 4&5/1994), whose boutique in Macao was destroyed in an arson attack the same day. (SWB)

MACEDONIA

On 17 May the Communication Ministry began closing down unlicenced private radio and television stations. Some 300 stations currently broadcast without permanent permits, around 40 of which have now been closed. (IFJ, FIEJ, SWB)

On 19 May Nevzat Halili, leader of the ethnic-Albanian Party for Democratic Prosperity (PDP), was sentenced to 18 months in prison for 'participating in a rally interfering with public authorities executing their duty'. The rally prevented police from raiding the Albanian-language university in Tetovo in February (*Index* 1/1995). On 23 and 24 May respectively Arben Rusi of the PDP and Musli Alimi, a former university professor from Kosovo, were each sentenced to eight months on the same charges. Halili was released on bail, pending appeal, on 6 June. It was reported on 31 May that Fadil Sulejman, the university's dean, had been released on bail, pending appeal. (OMRI, SWB)

On 27 June the Education Ministry announced a new draft law to allow private high schools to conduct classes in foreign languages. University tuition must still be held in Macedonian but teacher training may be conducted in minority languages. (OMRI)

MALAYSIA

Deputy home affairs minister Megat Ayob announced on 5

May that the Film Censorship Board (FCB) had banned the Indian film *Bombay* in March. The FCB said the film's portrayal of Hindu-Muslim rioting could have incited violence. (Reuter)

The housing and local government minister announced a ban on the import of video games that are 'detrimental to moral values' on 22 May. A ministerial committee has been set up to determine which games are to be banned. The move followed a Cabinet discussion on arresting 'the decline in moral values in young people'. (Reuter)

MOLDAVIA

Parliament voted in favour of a draft law on public meetings at the beginning of June, which severely restricts journalists' access to information, especially foreign journalists. Article 10 of the proposed law prohibits 'the access and participation of all foreigners in public meetings'. Other articles prohibit demonstrations from being held near government buildings, and stipulate that public meetings can only be held between the hours of 10am and 5pm. (RSF)

MOROCCO

Recent publication: *La Liberté de la Presse et de l'Information en Maroc* (A19/OMDH Morocco, June 1995, 360pp)

NAMIBIA

On 21 June the president's national security advisor, Peter Tshirumbu, gave a press conference in which he said that it is the 'patriotic duty' of everyone, including journalists, to share information with the Namibian Security Intelligence Agency (NSIA). The conference was held as a response to articles criticising NSIA harassment of journalists in the *Namibian*, *Die Republiken* and the *Windhoek Advertiser*. The government labelled the articles as 'fabrications'. (MISA)

On 8 June a government official entered the newsroom of the Namibian Broadcasting Corporation (NBC) and ordered that unedited footage of a presidential press conference be played in full on the evening television news. Although owned by the state, NBC is supposed to be editorially independent. (MISA, *Namibian*)

NEPAL

On 14 June a group of people protesting against the King's decision to dissolve Parliament assaulted Lekhnath Bhandari, an independent journalist, and smashed his camera. Thirteen people were hurt on 19 June during a demonstration held as part of a general strike by student groups opposing the dissolution. (RSF, Reuter)

Recent publication: *Rape for Profit: Trafficking of Nepali Girls and Women to India's Brothels* (HRW/Asia, July 1995, 90pp)

NIGERIA

A number of journalists have been detained in the wake of the alleged coup attempt in March (*Index* 3/1995). On 5 May George Mbah, a journalist with the weekly *Tell*, was arrested, apparently in connection with articles he has written about the coup. On 9 May Obi Ben Charles, of the weekly *Classic*, was arrested, followed on 16 May by Chido Onumah, a journalist with the daily *AM News*. (RSF)

Around 100 prominent human rights activists, including 10 journalists, were arrested in the run-up to the second anniversary of the annulled election of June 1993. Kunle Ajibade, editor-in-chief of the *News*, was detained by police who demanded that he reveal his sources for an article entitled 'No-one guilty: the Commission of Inquiry presents an empty file regarding suspects of the coup'. Chris Anyanwu (*Index* 3/1995), editor of *TSM* magazine, was arrested on 31 May. Ade Alawode, editor of the *Echo*, was arrested in early June. Among the human rights activists arrested are Olisa Agbakoba, president of the Nigerian Civil Liberties Organisation (CLO), Tunde Akanni, CLO campaign officer, Femi Falana, chairman of the National Association of Democratic Lawyers, Dr Beko Ransome-Kuti, chairman of the Campaign for Democracy, Alao Aka-Bashorun, president of the Democratic Alternative, and Onje Gye-Wado, a Democratic Alternative executive member. Agbakoba, Falana and Dr Beko Ransome-Kuti have since been released. (HRW, *Observer*)

Security forces used force to prevent all local and international journalists from entering the court where around 20 people accused of treason and plotting against the government were being tried (*Index* 3/1995). The secret trial, held at the Lagos garrison command, started on 5 June. On 20 June the trial of Shehu Yar Adua, the deputy of former head of state Olusegun Obasanjo, began. Obasanjo's own trial is thought to have started a few days earlier. Both men were charged with conspiracy. On 4 July it was reported that Obasanjo had been sentenced to 25 years in jail and 15 others sentenced to death. (Reuter, *Times*)

On 9 June the proscription order imposed on the Punch and Concord newspaper groups was extended for another six months (*Index* 4/1994, 2/1995). (Reuter, RSF)

Police raided the offices of the daily *AM News* in Lagos on 3 July, seized papers relating to police activities, and detained journalist Lekan Otufodunrin. Another *AM News* journalist, Babafemi Ojudu, was arrested without a warrant on 5 July, together with Olusesan Ekisola of the independent radio station Ray Power. (RSF)

Recent publication: *Fundamental Rights Denied — Report of the Trial of Ken Saro-Wiwa and Others* (A19 in association with the Bar Human Rights Committee of England and Wales and the Law Society of England and Wales, June 1995, 80pp)

PAKISTAN

The government threatened legal action against private news agencies and newspapers on 18 May for speculating about the future of the present chief of army staff, General Waheed. The authorities also called on the unnamed newspapers to 'tender unconditional apologies along with a commitment to act responsibly in future'. (Reuter)

An inquiry by the Human Rights Commission of Pakistan (HRCP) into the murder of Iqbal Masih (*Index* 3/1995) found that he was killed by accident rather than as a result of his advocacy on behalf of bonded labourers. The inquiry said he was killed by a man whom Iqbal saw having sex with a donkey. The Bonded Labour Liberation Front of Pakistan (BLLFP) maintain that Iqbal was a target for feudal landlords and carpet-industry owners. (Reuter)

The prime minister, Benazir Bhutto, stated 'emphatically' on 28 May that there are no plans to amend the blasphemy laws, but that their application will be improved. (SWB)

Aslam Gauthar, a journalist on *Khabrain*, was stabbed on 29 May in Multan, Punjab province. Gauhar received threatening 'phone calls after he wrote a report criticising a federal minister. Journalists, lawyers and opposition politicians protested against the attack on 4 June and called for the suspension of the Multan police chief. (RSF)

Zafar Yab Ahmed, a journalist with the *News* of Lahore, and Mohammad Salim, Fatima and Karamat Ali, workers with the Bonded Labour Liberation Front of Pakistan (BLLFP), were arrested in Lahore on 5 June. Zafar Yab was beaten at the time of his arrest and was accused of reporting the death of Iqbal Masih in such a way as to cause 'financial loss to the Pakistan business interest'. Zafar Yab and BLLF president Ehsanullah Khan were charged with 'sedition and collusion' with the Indian intelligence agency RAW. Zafar Yab's request for bail was refused. (A19, AI, CPJ)

A rocket-propelled grenade was fired at the offices of the *Nawa-e-Waqt* group of publications on 21 June (*Index* 3/1995). The attack occurred on the first day of a three-day mourning called by the Mohajir Qaumi Movement (MQM) following the gang-rape of a 16-year-old Mohajir girl by members of the ruling Pakistan People's Party (PPP) (*Index* 3/1995). On 25 June a rocket-propelled grenade was fired at the state-run television station in Karachi. There were no casualties. (Pakistan Press Foundation, CPJ)

The Sindh provincial government suspended the publication of six Karachi dailies on 29 June. *Public, Awam, Aghaz, Qaumi Akhbar, Evening Special* and *Parcham* were accused of spreading violence through sensationalist reporting. Faced with international protest and the threat of a nationwide journalists' strike, the banning order was lifted on 4 July. (Reuter, Pakistan Press Foundation)

The Communication Ministry issued a formal order on 3 July banning indefinitely the operation of all cellular, payphone and pager companies in Karachi. The suspension was ordered by the security services who claim that armed militants use the systems. (Reuter)

Over 300 people were killed in ethnic and political violence in Karachi during June. Over 950 have died so far this year. (Reuter)

Recent publications: *Executions under the Qisas and Diyat Ordinance* (AI, May 1995, 8pp); *The Continued Use of Bar Fetters and Cross Fetters* (AI, May 1995, 15pp)

PALESTINE (GAZA-JERICHO)

Sayed Abu Musameh, editor-in-chief of the pro-Hamas weekly *al-Watan*, was arrested on 13 May outside the paper's offices in Gaza by General Intelligence officers. He was tried by a secret State Security court and sentenced to two months' imprisonment for 'incitement against the Palestinian Authority'. The court also ordered that *al-Watan* be closed for three months. The order was lifted early on the order of Yasser Arafat in June. (RSF)

Recent publication: *Trial at Midnight: Secret, Summary, Unfair Trials in Gaza* (AI, June 1995, 25pp)

PAPUA NEW GUINEA

On 28 June the prime minister's senior media advisor, Franzalbert Joku, ordered the state-owned station Radio Kalang not to broadcast the popular *Roger Hau'ofa Talk Back Show*, which was to discuss the country's new local government system. Joku also said that the government would not allow a 'key government agency' to propagate information contrary to the majority view as expressed through Parliament. He added that critics should buy advertising time on commercial stations if they wished to make their opinions known. (RSF, Reuter)

PERU

Journalist Pedro Valdez Bernales (*Index* 6/1994) was freed from prison on 1 June after an appeals court overturned his conviction for having links to the Shining Path guerrillas. He had served two years of a 20-year sentence. The editor of *Hechos*, Javier Tuanama Valera (*Index* 4&5/1994, 1/1995) who is serving a 10-year sentence for links to the MRTA guerrillas, is reported to be in very poor health. (Instituto Prensa y Sociedad, FIP)

Congress passed an amnesty for military and police officers involved in human rights abuses during the campaign against the Shining Path on 14 June. The measure was introduced into Congress with no prior warning or public debate, and was passed within three hours of its appearance.

Congress leaders described it as an attempt at 'national reconciliation', but many human rights activists believe it will strengthen the climate of impunity for human rights violations. (Peru Support Group)

Radio Chota journalist David Passapera Portilla was imprisoned for disturbing the peace on 22 June after leaking documents relating to a judicial corruption investigation against the mayor of Chota. Mauro Vásquez Gonzales, also with Radio Chota, and Carlos Idrogo Bravo of the daily *La República*, also face a similar charge. (FIP)

Thieves broke into the offices of the Human Rights Commission in Lima on 8 July, stole office equipment and erased computer disks containing information on cases under investigation by the Commission. (*La República*, FIP)

PHILIPPINES

On 20 June journalist Florente Formento was injured in Cotabato, Mindanao, by two men who opened fire on him. Passers-by who came to his aid were threatened with a grenade. It is thought that Formento's stories on parliamentary elections in May provoked the attack. The mayor of the city has ordered an investigation into the incident. (RSF)

POLAND

President Walesa refused to sign the amended Radio and

TV Broadcasting Act on 13 June. By depriving the president of the right to appoint the chair of the National Radio and TV Broadcasting Council, he argued, the Act makes the Council a parliamentary, rather than a state, body. On 20 June the opposition Labour Union criticised what it sees as government attempts to undermine the independence of public broadcasters. (SWB)

A proposed new press law is set to place journalists under government regulation. The proposals include educational prerequisites for journalists, registration by a government-financed Press Council, and specific requirements for editors-in-chief. Although some amendments are expected, those provisions most likely to stay are the limits to foreign ownership (45 per cent) and corporate ownership (25 per cent). (Centre for Foreign Journalists)

ROMANIA

Sorin Rosca Stanescu, Adrian Patrusca and Tana Ardeleanu of the daily *Ziua* were charged with libel against authority in early June, in connection with articles accusing President Iliescu of having links to the KGB. If convicted, they face up to six years in jail. On 23 June *Ziua* reported that Ardeleanu had been videotaped meeting a reporter by two state security agents. On 26 June state security officials announced that the two agents had been suspended for infringements of professional rules, but denied they had been spying on Ardeleanu. (OMRI, Reuter)

It was reported in July that Marie-France Ionesco, daughter of the playwright Eugène Ionesco, has refused to allow any performances of her late father's plays, on which she holds the copyright, in protest at the country's human rights record. (*Independent*)

Recent publication: *Broken Commitment to Human Rights* (AI, May 1995, 43pp)

RUSSIA

On 17 May the State Duma published the text of a law on radioactive waste, which among other things guarantees the public the right to receive information promptly on the burial sites of toxic waste and on the radiation levels in any region. (SWB)

A bomb exploded in the editorial offices of the paper *Aleksinskie Vesti*, in Aleksin, Tula province, on 23 May. One person died and three were injured. (SWB)

The upper house of Parliament voted on 23 May to suspend the privatisation of state-owned television and radio companies (*Index* 2/1995). (Centre for Foreign Journalists)

Staff were locked out of the state broadcaster Ostankino on 8 June, because the lease on the building had expired, and has been transferred to Russian Public Television. An Ostankino executive accused the government of trying to 'strangle' the station. (SWB)

With the State Committee on the Press seeking to reduce federal subsidies by 148 billion rubles, and a massive drop in subscribers (from 220 million in 1990, to 20.8 million in 1994), many publications are close to the edge of extinction. Two important Moscow dailies, *Nezavisimaya Gazeta* and *Kuranty*, announced suspension of publication in June. (Centre for Foreign Journalists)

On 27 June a Russian court ordered the government paper *Rossiiskie Vesti* to print a retraction after it found the paper guilty of defaming the commercial group Most. It alleged in November 1994 that Most head, Vladimir Gusinsky [*see page 25*], was conspiring with the mayor of Moscow, Yuri Luzhkov, to overthrow President Yeltsin. (Jamestown *Monitor*)

Recent Publication: *Neither Jobs Nor Justice: State Discrimination Against Women in Russia* (HRW/Women's Rights Project, March 1995, 30pp)

RWANDA

On 12 May Isaie Niyoyita, the new editor of *Le Messager*, was served with a summons by the public prosecutor's office over unpublished articles that 'sowed hatred between the population and the government'. He was threatened with immediate imprisonment if they were published. The paper was subsequently seized as it was being printed later the same day. (RSF)

On 29 May police seized the latest issue of *Le Tribun du Peuple*, an independent weekly that often supports the government. Jean-Pierre Mugabe, the paper's editor, appeared on 30 May in the public prosecutor's office in Kigali. (RSF)

Ending a seminar on human rights and journalism in Kigali on 23 June, Rwandan journalists vowed to shun ethnic hatred and rebuild their country and profession. They appealed to the government to examine press laws, grant licences to private radio stations and recognise that reports of human rights violations are a national service. Major-General Paul Kagame, vice-president and defence minister, welcomed the proposals and promised to promote them. (Reuter)

Recent publications: *Crying out for Justice* (AI, 6 April 1995, 15pp); *Arming the Perpetrators of the Genocide* (AI, June 1995, 13pp)

SERBIA-MONTENEGRO

Serbia: Semi Radoncic of the independent weekly *Monitor* was sentenced to two months' imprisonment for libel in May over an article claiming that retired General Radomir Damjanovic had obtained an expensive car for 'little money'. He is the third *Monitor* journalist to be sentenced since the paper's launch. (OMRI)

On 10 June the culture minister announced that the Soros Foundation of Yugoslavia is no longer legally registered and therefore cannot finance projects. The Foundation has come under attack from pro-government media. It is not clear whether the Soros Open Society Fund is banned. (Alternative Information Network)

Kosovo: On 9 May Riza Greicevci of the paper *Bujku* was detained by police for several hours. His colleague Daut Maligi was briefly detained on 17 May and sports journalist Gani Kosumi was detained between 22 and 23 May, when his equipment and accreditation were confiscated. On 1 June *Bujku* editor Zeke Gacaj had his passport confiscated on the Macedonian border because he had made 'unauthorised' visits to Albania. (PEN)

In May Pal Krasnigi, secretary of the Independent Teachers' Trade Union of Kosovo was sentenced to two months in prison for organising a union branch meeting at Pristina Secondary School in November 1994. The school has not been used since 1990 owing to a boycott by Albanian students. (OMRI)

On 25 May 44 Albanian former policemen went on trial accused of setting up a shadow Kosovar police force. They claim they were tortured in custody and that they had merely set up an independent trade union to protect their rights. They face 10 years in jail if found guilty. The trial of a further 72 former policemen began on 29 May on charges of spying, stockpiling weapons and setting up a shadow interior ministry. (OMRI)

On 27 June Ramadan Mucolli, an ethnic-Albanian journalist, was arrested and detained for three days in Pristina. His tape recorder and passport were confiscated during a search of his flat. Mucolli was fired from Radio Pristina five years ago and has since worked for Albanian Radio and Television. (OMRI, SWB)

SINGAPORE

The National Arts Council (NAC) exempted a further nine theatre groups from prior censorship on 25 May. However they must still deposit a script with the NAC for its records and apply for a permit from the Public Entertainments Unit (Pelu) to stage a play. Furthermore the exemption can be withdrawn and a play stopped if it does not meet the NAC or Pelu's approval. The exemption is renewable annually, subject to conduct and performance. All plays must have 'artistic and literary merit' and be in 'good taste'. The guidelines preclude pieces which 'erode core moral values' (such as plays about homosexuality), 'subvert national security' or 'offend racial or religious sensibilities'. (Reuter)

SLOVAKIA

President Kovac criticised state television (STV) on 18 May, saying that the electronic media in Slovakia are not 'sufficiently plural or free'.

This was in response to the treatment of a short statement by Kovac, which STV broadcast late at night. The same day the head of programming at STV's Kosice studios barred the news team from filming a rally in support of Kovac, on the grounds that it was a 'repeat' of a rally held earlier in Bratislava. STV officials refused to allow Kovac to appear on television on 30 June, the day before the Papal visit to Slovakia, scheduling representatives of the Catholic Church to appear instead. (OMRI, SWB)

On 6 June the Petition Committee for the Preservation of Freedom of Speech called for the resignation of STV director Jozef Darmo over his pursuit of 'strongly anti-democratic activities' and his attacks on President Kovac. (SWB)

Journalists from the main daily papers *Pravda, Narodna Obrona* and *Praca* protested the government's information policy on 13 June. Since 18 March the government has severely restricted the amount of information it makes available to the press (*Index* 3/1995). Also on 13 June the government unveiled its plans for a new Slovak Information Agency, intended 'to promote Slovakia, especially abroad'. (SWB)

A draft law to limit the use of other languages in schools, state institutions and the media was approved by the Cabinet on 20 June. Strict guidelines affecting the language content of radio programmes have already been issued by the Culture Ministry, which will be acting as watchdogs for the new law. (OMRI, SWB)

SOUTH AFRICA

The ruling ANC has requested the public broadcaster, the South African Broadcasting Corporation (SABC), hand over 30 minutes of airtime each week for the ANC to put its message across in its own way. The ANC argues that the people need to know what the government is doing to improve their lives. (*Southern Africa Report*)

In May the SABC announced plans to use English on its public television sevice and to include Afrikaans with nine ethnic languages on a channel directed at low-income rural viewers. Several large Afrikaans businesses have since threatened to withdraw advertising from the SABC. (*Southern Africa Report*)

On 4 May police raided the right-wing radio station Radio Donkerhoek (*Index* 3/1995), which continues to broadcast without a licence. A spokesman for the Pretoria-based station says they are standing up for 'each volk's right to freedom of speech'. (Freedom of Expression Institute)

The South African Police Service (SAPS) warned on 18 May that they will continue to seize adult magazines until the Publications Act is amended. The warning followed seizures of *Hustler* (*Index* 3/1995), *Penthouse, Playboy, Eros* and *Men Only*. (Freedom of Expression Institute)

In a unanimous ruling on 7 June the Constitutional Court ruled that capital punishment is unconstitutional. The ruling was greeted by prisoners on death row with singing and applause. (*Times, Guardian, Southern Africa Report*)

Recent publication: *Threats to a New Democracy: Continuing Violence in KwaZulu-Natal* (HRW/Africa, May 1995, 37pp)

SOUTH KOREA

Park Chang-hee, a history professor, was arrested under the National Security Law on 26 April and accused of meeting with a 'pro-North Korea' contact in Japan. Reports suggest that he has been ill-treated during interrogation, beaten, deprived of sleep and forced to consume alcohol. (PEN)

French reporter and photographer Pierre Bessard was refused entry to South Korea on 10 May. Officials said Bessard had violated the National Security Law by visiting North Korea prior to his arrival. On 30 May the French Foreign Ministry informed Bessard that he has been banned from South Korea. (RSF)

On 6 June police arrested 13 trade union leaders with Korea Telecom in a raid on Myongdong Cathedral and Chogye-sa Temple in Seoul.

The arrests were part of an effort to prevent the formation of a new dissident labour group, the Democratic Trade Union Council. (*Financial Times*)

Recent publications: *Letters From Prisoners and Their Families* (AI, May 1995, 13pp); *Concerns Relating to Freedom of Expression and Opinion* (AI, June 1995, 11pp)

SRI LANKA

Kithulagama Seelankara, a leading Buddhist monk, was shot dead by gunmen from the Liberation Tigers of Tamil Eelam (LTTE) on 26 May in the north-central Polonnaruwa district. Seelankara had recently spoken out against government proposals to devolve power to the mainly Hindu Tamils. (Reuter)

President Kumaratunga again threatened the press with tighter censorship on 28 May (*Index* 2/1995). She told reporters at the opening of the National Information Centre that 'We will not kill journalists and drop them by air on the beaches,' but demanded that reporters show responsibility in their reporting of the ongoing conflict with Tamil secessionists. The information minister said at the beginning of June that censorship may be introduced if papers publish 'ethnically oriented material'. (Reuter, FIEJ)

Newspapers published photographs of five mutilated bodies found in Kurunegala district on 5 July. This follows the discovery of 11 bodies floating in a lake outside Colombo. The bodies are believed to be those of abducted Tamil youths. (Reuter)

Recent publication: *Reports of Extrajudicial Executions During May 1995* (AI, June 1995, 6pp)

SUDAN

Adilah Al-Zaybaq, a leading women's activist and journalist, has disappeared after being arrested by security forces in Khartoum on 20 March. She was arrested after obtaining an entry visa to the USA to attend a women's conference. Al-Zaybaq was a leading member of the banned Sudan Women's Union and edited its underground magazine, *Sawt Al-Mara*. (*Sudan Update*)

Sadiq al-Mahdi, leader of the Umma Party and prime minister until a coup in 1989, was arrested on 16 May for 'involvement in subversive activities'. At least 25 others with connections to the Umma Party were also detained at around the same time in Khartoum and Port Sudan. The crackdown appears to be in retaliation for al-Mahdi's outspoken criticism of the government in a speech given on 10 May. (AI, *Sudan Update*)

SWAZILAND

The minister of broadcasting, information and tourism, Prince Khuzulwandle Dlamini, has announced the kingdom's first draft media law. The legislation is designed to fight harassment and intimidation of journalists by government officials. (Human Rights Committee of South Africa)

Four senior employees of the *Swazi Observer* and the *Times of Swaziland* have been charged with contravening the Books and Newspapers Act by publishing and printing their respective newspapers without certificates of registration. Both papers have been publishing without certificates for

over 30 years. (MISA)

TAIWAN

In May the Chinese authorities pressured the UN to deny six Taiwanese women's groups accreditation at the UN Women's Conference in Beijing, unless they register as part of the Chinese delegation. On 18 May the European Parliament passed a resolution calling on China to allow women from Taiwan and Tibet to attend the conference. (*Taiwan Communique*)

TAJIKISTAN

Mirzo Salimov, correspondent for the Moscow-based Tajik paper *Charogi Ruz* (*Index* 3/1995), was released on 24 May, having been charged under the Criminal Code with 'war propaganda', 'organisational activity directed towards commission of especially dangerous state crimes and participation in an anti-government organisation', and 'violating the equal rights of nationalities and races'. Pending investigation, Salimov may not leave the country. (AI, CPJ)

TANZANIA

Freelance journalist Edina Ndejembi (*Index* 3/1995) was acquitted of obstructing the police by Moshi magistrates on 26 June. Sam Makila, the editor of the Kiswahili daily *Majira*, and the paper's publishers, Rashidi Mbuguni and Richard Nyaulawa, have been charged with sedition and withholding information after Makila refused to reveal the source of a story on the government's planned acquisition of radar equipment. (MISA)

Oliver Msuya and Yasin Sadiki, publisher and editor respectively of the independent weekly *Shaba*, were arrested on 6 July, after *Shaba* published a leaked letter from the interior minister in which he says he has been instructed to 'curb the activities' of a leading opposition politician. Also in early July, the home affairs minister is reported to have banned all political cartoons. Many publications immediately responded by using far more cartoons than usual. (MISA, Reuter)

TIBET

The authorities banned monks from leaving their monasteries on 6 July, the day chosen to mark the 60th birthday of the Dalai Lama. Abbots were ordered to enforce the ban on two prayers, 'Words of Truth', written by the Dalai Lama, and 'Long Life', both of which praise Tibetan courage and call for self-determination. (*Observer*)

Recent publication: *Persistent Human Rights Violations in Tibet* (AI, May 1995, 52pp)

TUNISIA

The travel ban imposed on Moncef Marzouki (*Index* 3/1994, 1/1995, 3/1995) has been lifted and his passport has been returned to him. (SWB)

Mohamed Kilani (*Index* 2/1995), member of the Tunisian Workers' Communist Party (PCOT) and editor of the suspended left-wing paper *El Badil*, was sentenced to five years' imprisonment on 27 April for possessing a leaflet which contained a caricature of the former minister of the interior. He also received a two-year sentence in February for supporting an unauthorised association and holding unauthorised meetings. (AI)

Recent publication: *Aicha Dhaouadi, Prisoner of Conscience* (AI, June 1995, 5pp)

TURKEY

In the spring the Istanbul State Security Court banned the book *Genocide as a Question of National and International Law — The 1915 Armenian Event and its Consequences*, written by US academic Vahakn Dadrian. A Turkish translation of this book was published by the Belge Publishing House whose director, Ayse Zarakolu, now faces prosecution for separatist propaganda. Zarakolu is already in prison for publishing *The Armenian Taboo* by French author Yves Ternon. The court has also instituted legal proceedings against Abdulkadir Konuk, the book's translator, and journalist Ragip Zarakolu, who wrote a preface to it. (CCPJ)

Twenty-six of the 30 issues of the pro-Kurdish daily *Yeni Politika* (*Index* 3/1995) that have been released since it started publishing on 13 April have been confiscated by the Istanbul State Security Court for 'separatist propaganda' and promoting 'discrimination between people of different races, religion, regions or social classes'. On 2 June Sanh Ekin, the paper's news director, was reportedly taken into custody. (*Kurdistan News, Yeni Politika*, A19)

On 16 May Hidir Goktas, a parliamentary reporter for Reuter, journalist Metin Gulbay, and publisher Hasan Basri Ciplak, were found guilty of 'spreading separatist propaganda' in their book *Yeni Dunya Dezeni ve Turkiye* (The New World Order and Turkey). The book quotes Kurdish parliamentarian Halip Dicle as saying that the Kurds are 'in the process of forming a nation'. All three are free pending appeal. (CCPJ)

Ahmet Altan, a former editorial writer with the daily *Milliyet*, appeared in court on 17 May to face a charge of promoting racial, social or religious discrimination in a satirical article he wrote about an imaginary country called 'Kurdiye'. The charge carries a maximum sentence of six years in prison. (RSF)

On 2 June Salih Bal, former editor-in-chief of the Kurdish-owned newspaper *Medya Gunesi* (Sun of the Medes), his wife Hilal Okumus, Mehmet Sanri, correspondent, and Zelal Boga, a telephone operator for the paper, were arrested at their homes in Istanbul. They were taken to the anti-terror branch of Istanbul police headquarters where it is feared they may face torture. (AI)

On 16 June the Istanbul State Security Court prosecutor indicted 99 intellectuals who claimed to be publishers of the book *Freedom of Thought and Turkey*, a collection of 11 articles by various authors including Yaşar Kemal. Kemal's article in the book accuses the government of suppressing Kurds in southeastern Turkey. A total of 1,080 artists, writers, journalists and trade union leaders have declared themselves responsible for publishing the book in support of Kemal and Erdal Oz, the book's real publisher. An additional 50,000 have signed petitions stating their support. The prosecutor is demanding prison sentences of at least four years for each of the defendants. (*Info-Turk*)

Sabahat Varol, a journalist with the magazine *Devrimci Genclik* (Revolutionary Youth), was detained on 20 June as she left the People's Law Office in Istanbul. The Office has acted as defence counsel in many prosecutions involving charges of membership of the illegal armed organisation DHKP-C, formerly known as *Devrimci Sol* (Revolutionary Left). (AI)

The TV stations Kanal-D, Show Television and Kanal-6 were banned for 24 hours on 1 July after the broadcasting High Council found that they had 'violated the principle of respect for public morals, the Turkish family structure and modesty'. (SWB)

Recent publications: *Mothers of the 'Disappeared' Take Action* (AI, May 1995, 15pp); *Paroles Interdites* (Forbidden Words) (RSF, June 1995, 56pp)

UGANDA

Henry Mirima, editor-in-chief of the monthly *Exposure*, and Nassar Seebagala were arrested following the non-appearance in court of *Citizen* editor, Lawrence Kiwanuka, on 19 May (*Index* 3/1995). Mirima and Seebagala were standing security for Kiwanuka. (RSF)

A new Press Law enacted by Parliament in late May stipulates that editors must hold a degree in journalism. Only three of the country's 15 publications satisfy the requirement, and a number of journalists have vowed to defy the new law. (*East Africa Standard*)

UKRAINE

The Presidium of the Crimean Parliament withdrew accreditation from journalist Hrihoriy Yoffe on 13 June, alleging that he had infringed Ukraine's mass media and information laws. (SWB)

Russian speakers in Donetsk picketed the town hall on 27 June to protest against the cancellation of the Russian-language programme *Choice*. Ukraininan nationalist groups had criticised the programme for 'infringing Ukraine's sovereignty', particularly in a recent series of programmes about World War II. (SWB)

Recent publication: *The Death Penalty: A Cruel, Inhuman and Degrading Punishment* (AI, July 1995, 16pp)

INDEX INDEX

UNITED KINGDOM

On 12 May a Kuwaiti princess, Souad al-Sabah, won a High Court order forcing the withdrawal from sale of a book about Mark Thatcher's business interests. The princess objected to claims in *Thatcher's Gold*, by Paul Halloran and Mark Hollingsworth, that she had been a mistress of Saddam Hussein and that she had arranged business contracts for Thatcher. The book has since been taken off the market for revision. (*Guardian, Independent*)

Under new plans unveiled by Home Secretary Michael Howard on 16 May, defendants in court must disclose their defence to the prosecution in advance, while the prosecution will have to reveal to the defence only a limited amount of material. At present the defence can usually keep its entire case under wraps while the prosecution must disclose virtually everything. (*Guardian*)

On 23 May the Government committed itself to implementing new media ownership rules under which newspaper groups controlling less than 20 per cent of total national circulation will be allowed to control up to 15 per cent of the total television market; national newspapers with more than 20 per cent of the market will be restricted to a 20 per cent stake in one regional independent television franchise; there will be an immediate relaxation of radio ownership limits; and no single company shall be permitted to own more than 10 per cent of the total national media. (*Guardian, Independent*)

On 30 May two journalists for the *Big Issue North West*, Ursula Wills-Jones and Justin Cooke, were arrested while covering a protest against opencast mining. They were held for 13 hours and subsequently charged with trespass under the Criminal Justice Act (CJA), even though they were attending the event in a purely journalistic capacity. They are believed to be the first journalists to be charged under the CJA. (NUJ)

The nationwide book and magazine chain W H Smith withdrew from sale all copies of the video *Executions* on 19 June because of the film's explicit subject matter. Another chain, John Menzies, announced that it would not be reordering further copies when stocks ran out. The video contains documentary footage of 21 executions, including a woman being stoned to death in Somalia, beheadings in Saudi Arabia and the bodies of torture victims in former Yugoslavia. It was passed by the British Board of Film Classification with an 18 certificate. (*Independent*)

A one-minute advert by Amnesty International has been banned by the Radio Authority under the Broadcasting Act 1990, which states that groups cannot advertise if their work is 'wholly or mainly of a political nature'. The ban was upheld in the High Court on 4 July. Amnesty argued that their work was humanitarian and that the definition of 'political' was too broad (*Index* 3/1995). (*Independent, Financial Times*)

UNITED NATIONS

The book *Vision of Hope*, commissioned by the UN to coincide with its 50th anniversary in June, had several passages cut prior to publication. A quote by Tibet's exiled leader, the Dalai Lama, was excised, along with a passage citing pressure brought by UN officials on non-governmental organisations that were seeking to publicly name countries with poor human rights records. All the book's contributing authors have withdrawn their names from their articles in protest, although the UN denies that the cuts were intended as censorship. (Reuter, *Statesman*)

USA

In April the Republican National Committee demanded that Brooklyn artists Nora Ligorano and Marshall Reese cease their 'unauthorised use' of the 'Contract with America' logo and text on the artists' Contract with America underwear (*right*). (American Civil Liberties Union)

The Supreme Court ruled on 19 May that the organisers of Boston's St Patrick's Day parade were entitled to exclude homosexual and bisexual groups who wanted to take part. The Court decided that rulings by a Massachusetts state court in 1992 and 1993, that gay

UNITED KINGDOM - USA

groups must be allowed to participate, violated the First Amendment rights of the parade organisers. (*Irish Times*)

In a landmark case a New York state judge ruled on 26 May that the Prodigy Internet server is legally a publisher and therefore subject to the laws of libel and legally responsible for material carried on its bulletin boards (BBS). The ruling came in a suit for damages by the investment group Stratton Oakmont over critical comments on a Prodigy BBS about the company. Prodigy argues that it is not a publisher, but a 'common carrier', analogous to a telephone company or bookshop. (*Guardian*)

The House Judiciary Committee approved the proposed Comprehensive Terrorism Prevention Act (*Index* 3/1995) on 20 June. The bill, which has already been through the Senate, contains expanded surveillance provisions for federal agencies to conduct 'roving' wiretaps (covering several telephones without separate court orders) and to gain access to hotel, credit card and telephone bills. Most controversially, the bill contains a so-called 'habeas corpus reform' provision, limiting all condemned federal and state prisoners — whether convicted of terrorist offences or not — to one appeal in federal courts, which must be made within one year of the conviction. (*Los Angeles Times*)

The House of Representatives approved a constitutional amendment on 28 June to allow Congress and the states to prohibit desecration of the US flag. The amendment now goes before the Senate and then to the individual states for ratification. (PEN)

House leader Newt Gingrich challenged the Communications Decency Act (*Index* 3/1995) in June. The proposed Act imposes sentences of two years in prison and fines of up to $100,000 for anyone who places sexually explicit material which can be accessed by minors, on the Internet. Gingrich said the measure was 'clearly a violation of free speech, and a violation of the right of adults to communicate with each other'. (*Guardian*)

The Supreme Court ruled on 29 June that a public university cannot refuse funding to a student-run religious publication. The Court decided that the University of Virginia had violated the First Amendment rights of Ronald Rosenberger, a student who wanted funding for his Christian magazine *Wide Awake*. The University's argument, that to subsidise the magazine would violate the constitutional requirement on church-state separation, was narrowly rejected by five votes to four. (Reuter)

On 10 July President Clinton announced his support for the application of 'v-chip' technology (*Index* 1&2/1994), which would allow adults to block reception of television programmes that were unsuitable for children. The v-chip proposal is contained in a broad telecommunications bill currently before the Senate, which does away with existing restrictions on media and cross-media ownership. (Reuter, *Guardian*)

Mumia Abu-Jamal (*Index* 2/1995), the journalist sentenced to death for his alleged part in the killing of a police officer in 1981, is to be executed on 17 August. The governor of Pennsylvania, Thomas Ridge, signed the death warrant on 1 June, four days before Abu-Jamal's Post-Conviction Review Appeal

Contract with America Underwear

was due to be filed. (FIP)

Recent publication: *Blinding Laser Weapons* (HRW/Arms Project, May 1995, 16pp)

VANUATU

In mid-June the prime minister's office banned circulation of all information on the resumption of French nuclear testing on the Mururoa Atoll. The ban not only affects local material but also foreign pieces broadcast by Radio Vanuatu. The government also banned a demonstration against the testing, planned for 24 June. (RSF)

YEMEN

Ibrahim Hussein, a journalist for *Al-Ayyam*, was detained on 27 May. He was conditionally released a few days later. (RSF)

Ali al-Sahrari, a journalist with the Yemeni Socialist Party paper *al-Thrawi*, has been detained without charge since 28 May. On the same day Hicham Said Salem, editor-in-chief of the government daily *14th of October*, was arrested by political security officers. (RSF)

Hussein Muhammed Nasser, editor-in-chief of the defunct weekly *al-Jadid*, Fadl Ali Mubarak, journalist with *al-Wahdawi*, and Ali Abdullah Munser, Abin correspondent for the SABA news agency (*Index* 3/1995), were released in late April. Hussein Muhammed Nasser and Fadl Ali Mubarak were subsequently rearrested and then released on 31 May. Saleh Ali, a cartoonist for *al-Wahdawi*, was also released the same day. (RSF, CPJ)

ZAIRE

Two journalists from the paper *Le Point Zaire*, Belmonde Magloire Coffi Missinhoun and Nestor-Marie Mazangu Mbuilu, are still in prison following their detention on 1 and 18 April respectively. They are charged with 'contempt, defamation and making injurious charges' in an article criticising the attorney-general and the former head of a private airline. At least nine other journalists and their contacts have reported detention or harassment in the last two months. (RSF)

ZAMBIA

Two journalists with the *Post*, Fred M'membe and Masautso Phiri, were detained on 19 June and charged with defaming the president in an article alleging that he had a Zairean mistress. The pair were released on bail the following day. (MISA)

Weston Handu, an intelligence officer working for President Chiluba, appeared in court on 26 June on a charge of 'conveying information to unauthorised people' at the *Post* newspaper. The information contained a letter from the Mansa office of the Zambian Intelligence Security Service (ZISS) which claimed that 'a National Campaign Committee for the Re-Election of President Chiluba has been formed and is pre- pared to assassinate the former president'. (MISA)

***

General publications: *Spotlight On: Human Rights Violations in Times of Armed Conflict* (Humanitarian Law Center, Belgrade, 1995, 157pp); *Reporters Sans Frontières 1995 Report* (RSF, 1995, 320pp); *Violence* (UNESCO, June 1995, 71pp); *Second Memorandum to Governments on the Revised Draft Platform for Action of the Fourth UN World Conference on Women* (AI, June 1995, 9pp); *Honoring Human Rights and Keeping the Peace: Lessons from El Salvador, Cambodia and Haiti* (ed Alice H Henkin, Aspen Institute Justice and Society Program, 1995, 172pp)

We congratulate those of our contributors, often writing in difficult and dangerous situations, who have been given this year's Hellman/Hammett Awards: Aïcha Lemsine, Ken Saro-Wiwa, Mumia Abu-Jamal, Lindsey Collen, Hodi Khosandi and Nguyen Van Ho. The awards are given annually to writers who have been targets of political persecution.

Compiled by: Anna Feldman, Jason Garner, Kathryn Thal (Africa); Nathalie de Brogio, Adam Newey (Americas); Nicholas McAulay, Atanu Roy, Sarah Smith (Asia); Colin Isham (central Asia); Laura Bruni, Robin Jones, Vera Rich (eastern Europe and CIS); Michaela Becker, Philippa Nugent (Middle East); Daniel Brett, Jamie McLeish (western Europe) ❏